God's Footprints
On a Farm Boy

By
Lou Nicholes

A Missionary With Word of Life For 50 Years

Lou Nicholes
Prov. 3:5, 6

God's Footprints On a Farm Boy
by Lou Nicholes

Printed in the United States of America

ISBN 9781625093486

Deanna Ream – Copy Editor of the manuscript
Proof Reading by Maureen McCarron and Barbara Teboe

www.xulonpress.com

Forward

I've had the high privilege of knowing Lou Nicholes since I was a young man. His life story serves as a fresh reminder that as we faithfully serve God, His footprints are evident in our lives with every single step we take. It's only God who can move a young man from a humble background on a farm in the Midwest, to impact the lives of thousands of young people in the United States and literally around the world.

When I think of Lou and his dear family, the words faithfulness and fruitfulness immediately come to mind. Whether serving local church Bible clubs, leading missions trips, or representing Word of Life Asia, Lou is all in...all the time. While only eternity will reveal the extent of his ministry, it is known that at least 150 people are on the mission field today as a result.

My prayer is that this story will challenge you to serve the Lord faithfully with every fiber of your being. God wants to use you to impact this world for Him. Don't miss His footprints and leading in your own life.

Don Lough, Jr., Executive Director Word of Life Fellowship, Inc.

Introduction

L ou Nicholes and I are the personification of I Corinthians 1:26-31. Paraphrased in my words, "God doesn't choose to use many great intellects, wise or noble men, so he uses very ordinary people who see themselves as a 'nobody.' God uses 'nobodies' to do his great work because when something great is achieved through them, they do not try to take the credit, they give it all to the Lord, knowing that it is GOD who achieves it through them."

I have been known to refer to Lou as "Bulldog Nicholes" because once he became convinced God wanted him to do something, whether he was capable or not, he would try to do it and do it well. It would make no difference whether he had experience at it or not, he would try and try and try until he had success. He is one of the most determined men I know.

Because of this spirit, God has given him success in whatever it was God gave him to do. While Lou was our Mid-West regional director, he was responsible for more than 250 Bible Clubs and more than 1,000 local church lay leaders. He would often see somewhere between one and two thousand young people coming to faith in Jesus Christ during one year's time.

Though I was the one to birth the Word of Life Bible Club ministry, we always worked together as a team of men. No one on our staff made more significant contributions to the betterment and development of the Bible Club ministry, than did Lou. When Lou came on our staff we were very much in the "pioneer mode" of development. He knew what it was to put endless hours into a project and always had significant ideas on organizing any project with which he was associated.

This story of Lou's life is one of humble beginnings. It is the story of a life wholly given over to serving the Lord. It is a story of faithfulness to the cause of bringing thousands of young people to Jesus Christ.

As one to whom Lou answered for forty years in the ministry, I look back on my experience as his leader and say, **"Well done, good and faithful servant, great will be your reward!"** – Paul Bubar, Word of Life Fellowship

Appreciation

I have many people to thank for making the writing of this book possible. First of all are my wonderful parents, Lester and Mary Nicholes, who brought me into this world and are now residing in their new mansion in Glory. I believe my salvation experience is a direct result of my godly mother's prayers. Words alone cannot express my heart felt thanks for my dear wife, Thelma, who has been my partner, helper, lover, and encourager for over fifty years. My children Steve, Mike, and Beth have not only brought me great joy but have been great helpers and encouragers, starting at a very early age. They worked very hard in our office and print shop, were a vital part of our many evangelistic roundup opportunities, ministered with us in our family weekend ministries, helped with the tract ministry, advertised, recruited and went with us on several short-term mission trips. We could have never begun to do all we did without them.

Jack Wyrtzen opened the door of ministry opportunities around the world by inviting my wife and I to be missionaries with Word of Life in 1962. It was his godly example and enthusiastic roll model in evangelism and discipleship that has motivated me in much of my missionary activity over the years. He was always interested in me as a person, and praying for me for which I am very thankful. I praise the Lord for Paul Bubar, who has not only been my boss but my best friend for most of my years in Word of Life. He not only made me feel as a vital part of the team but allowed me to use my pioneering spirit in the development of new programs and materials.

I owe a debt of gratitude to Ray Pritchard, who is a well known Bible Conference speaker, teacher and author of many books as well as the founder and director of <u>www. KeepBelieving.Com</u>. He is the one who encouraged me to publish my devotional commentaries and put them up on the internet. I now have the whole Bible available on <u>www. Family-Times.Net</u>. In addition, I am especially thankful for many churches and individuals who have faithfully prayed for us and supported us financially for over a half century. And last but not least, thanks to all of you that have been good friends and co-workers over these many years.

Contents

Forward.... v

Introduction...vii

Appreciation..ix

1. Early Life 13

2. Adolescent and Teen Years 16

3. Life Choices 21

4. After High School Graduation 24

5. Army Days 28

6. First Missionary Journey.................................33

7. Farm Boy Meets Farm Girl..............................38

8. Steps of Faith in the Ministry..........................44

9. Bible Club Years 50

10. Does God Really Answer Prayer?....................55

11. Evangelistic Events 58

12. Short Term Missions 63

13. Life Threatened 69

14. Farm Boy Goes to Russia 74

15. Family Ministry 79

16. Asked to be an Asia Representative 84

Dear Dad and Mom.... 89

Comment.... 95

Early Life

I am sure that my mother never imagined the day she gave birth to a 9 lb. 8 oz. blond headed, brown-eyed boy that he would one day stare down a gun barrel held by a masked man on the other side of the world. Especially when the man raised the gun a few inches over his head and fired it three times, then barked the orders that he get out of the van he was in and walk to the back of it where another masked man held a bundle of rope. However, I am jumping ahead of my story, so let's drop back to where it all started in a small farming community in the hills of southeastern Ohio.

Lester and Mary Nicholes lived in a rented farmhouse on a small farm near Layman, Ohio. Layman was a very small town located in a rural area of southeastern Ohio. They lived next door to David and Mary Ann Nicholes, who were Lester's parents. Together they operated a 120 acre farm with cattle, pigs, sheep, and chickens. My dad (Lester) also owned a school bus to supplement his income from the farm and was paid by the school board to deliver children to local schools in the township

August 31, 1933 was a very exciting day in this remote farmhouse. The only medical doctor in the area was coming. The only son Wayne, who was 11 years old at the time, was sent to his grandparents for the day. Later in the day the doctor arrived, and in a few hours the sounds of a new baby were coming from the house. Soon mom and dad announced that it was a boy, and his name was Louis.

In those days no one in the rural area of Ohio had electricity. This meant no indoor plumbing, and an outhouse was behind each home. The house was heated with a wood and coal stove. All cooking was also done with a wood stove, and all water was heated on the stove. Lights which were all kerosene, and water was supplied by a dug well or a cistern that caught water from the roof. This was dispensed with a hand pump. This is the way it was in my house until I was in high school.

We raised all our garden produce, had fruit trees, and butchered our own meat. We had a car, but were limited in travel during the winter months because many of the roads were dirt and often impassable. We had to go to a city, which was about 25 miles away for shopping. My parents only went for groceries or other supplies about every 6 to 8 weeks, and then it was usually for salt, pepper, sugar or spices. We truly were pretty self-sufficient and independent of the outside world for most things. According to today's standards we would be very poor, but at that time it was very normal living for a farming community.

When I was six years old, dad bought a 100 acre farm about 6 miles away, near the town of Bartlett, with a population of around 200 people. It had a small grocery store, a hardware store, a bank, and a few other buildings. It also had a small church and a school building that included both elementary and high school. This is where I attended school from first grade through high school. There were 21 in my graduating class. In a school that size we knew everyone almost like family.

My dad wanted me to be a farmer, so he encouraged me by giving me my own sheep, pigs, and beef cattle. My brother and I worked with dad on the farm. My responsibilities increased when my brother graduated from high school and joined the Merchant Marines during the Second World War. So I was left to work with my dad on the farm during my adolescent and teen years. After the war my brother never came back to the farm.

At first we farmed with horses; later on we had a tractor. I had lots of experience hoeing corn, shocking wheat, pitching hay, as well as raising animals. When I was just a small boy, my dad would often give me an incentive to work hard. I can remember being in the field hoeing corn with him when he would say, "If you can get to the end of your row sooner than I can mine, I will treat you to a double dip ice cream cone;" and I would just make the weeds fly.

We raised pumpkins in our corn field, and each fall my mother would have a goal of baking 100 pumpkin pies. When I was a teenager, dad and I would be in the field working in the afternoon and he would say, "Let's go to the house for a snack. I think mother is baking some pies." We would come into the house hungry, and mother would cut a pie in half. I would eat one half, and dad would eat the other half.

It was a great way to grow up learning how to do many things. My mother always raised a large garden and canned the produce, which helped train me for later on. We worked hard, but we had time for fun as well. After a busy week, we would sometimes invite the neighbors to come to our house for a cookout, make ice cream with our hand cranked freezer and play yard games until it was dark. Then while the adults sat around and visited, the children would often chase lightening bugs and put them in a bottle, seeing who could collect the most.

> *"When you eat the labor of your hands, You*
> *shall be happy, and it shall be well with you."*
> Psalm 128:2 NKJV

This verse was evident in our home even before I became a Christian.

Adolescent and Teen Years

For many it is hard to imagine growing up in a rural community without electricity, and many of the modern conveniences that we enjoy today. However, I wouldn't trade the many great experiences I enjoyed and the practical lessons of life that I learned, in those early days on the farm. My mother and dad thought we had just about the best possible life there was to live and taught me to enjoy the simple things of life, as we worked in the fields, milked the cows, fed the chickens and slopped the pigs.

When we moved to Bartlett I started first grade. We lived one-half mile from the school on a dirt road. Part of the year the road was impassable because of either mud or snow. This meant that usually I had to walk to school. Eventually they graveled the road and then the school bus would come by. However, I was the first one on the bus in the morning and the last one off at night so most of the time I would still walk. I liked school, but my favorite time was recess when we played marbles, hide and seek, dodge ball, and later softball, volleyball, and basketball.

Once I entered junior high and high school, I made the basketball team and spent a lot of my time either playing or practicing the game. By that time one of my jobs at home was milking two old cows by hand. We often had a dozen or more cats around the barn to keep the rats and mice population thinned out and these cats would watch me milk and beg for milk. I remember squirting them good to keep them at a distance before I would give them a nice big dish of warm milk. We milked these two cows for our own milk, cream, and butter, as well as selling the milk to the neighbors.

My dad said I could play basketball as long as the cows got milked morning and evening. Once in a while he would do it for me if we had an "away" game. During one of my junior high years, we were playing in the championship game of our County Basketball Tournament, and the score was tied with 1 minute to play. I fouled out and had to sit on the bench. I didn't think I really committed the foul and just sat there getting angrier. The final buzzer blew, and we lost the game by one point. I got up from the bench angry and walked up behind the referee, who was holding the ball in front of him. I stopped in front of him and hit the ball with my fist, and the ball came up and hit him in the face. I walked off to the shower room, took a shower, and got on the bus for home. I didn't realize it, but he had written down the number on my jersey.

The next day the principal of our school called me to his office and asked me if I hit the basketball that went into the referee's face. I told him I did. He talked with me for awhile, and then he gave me some stationary and told me to sit there and write an apology to the referee. He said he would come back and check it when I was finished. I sat there for an hour with the intention of doing nothing. He came back about an hour later and when he found out I had done nothing, he said, "Okay, I will give you another hour to write the letter, and if when I come back, you have not written it, I will call your parents." I knew the results would not be good when they found out, so I wrote the letter. I did some serious thinking about my angry spirit, and it turned out to be a great lesson for me to learn how to control my anger. I have thought about this incident several times throughout my life when I have been tempted to get angry about something I didn't like, or when I have seen someone else get angry and try to take things into his own hands.

During these years of growing up on the farm we worked hard all week. My dad always told me that he didn't think hard work ever hurt anyone. Then on Saturday night, he would always take me with him to our little town. He would sit around and visit with neighbors and other farmers in the area for a couple of hours or so. Keep in mind that in those days there was no such thing as TV to watch on Saturday night. While they were visiting, I would play with neighbor boys and friends. One of the games we often played was called "cinch." It was played with traditional playing cards, but there was no gambling involved. It was just for fun!

I remember one night some of us had a wild and rather ambitious idea. It was a Saturday night, and the Eastern Star and Mason Lodges of the area were having a special gathering, and everyone came in formal dress. The meeting was held on the second floor of a large hall in town. It was a hot summer evening, and all the windows were large and wide open to take advantage of any air that was stirring. A few days before this some of us boys had observed a huge hornets' nest attached to a small branch along the road. We got the idea of sneaking up to it after dark, and sticking a cork in the hole in the bottom of it. Then we clipped off the small branch that held the nest. You guessed it! In the dark we carried the nest to the large lodge hall. There was a fire escape on the back that took us near a window where this large gathering was being held.

While this meeting was going on, we sneaked up the fire escape, pulled the plug on the hornets' nest, and heaved it into the center of the circle where they were meeting. You can picture how mad those hornets were, and it didn't take long for them to come pouring out of that nest. You can also imagine how fast people began to scatter. It didn't take long for the people to come pouring out of that second-floor building. However the boys who did this dastardly deed had already fled the area. The lodge members looked everywhere to find out who did this, but couldn't find anyone. The boys had sworn themselves to secrecy, and as far as I know, this may be the first time anyone has "let the cat out of the bag" in over 60 years.

Two important organizations that I enjoyed greatly and my parents encouraged me in when I was growing up were the 4-H club, and the Boy Scouts. In the 4-H club, we met in different homes and worked on various projects such as gardening, and animal care. I had my own registered Herford cows, and Berkshire hogs that I entered into various contests. One of my favorite times of year was in the fall when we would display them at both the Barlow and Washington County Fairs.We would actually go with them, and sleep in the animal barns at night during this fair time. We would spend hours and hours of grooming them, and getting them ready for show time in order to try to get a red or blue ribbon.

Many of my school friends were involved with me in the Boy Scouts. We worked hard on merit badges and had a sash we wore with our uniform as we advanced to the various levels, of which I achieved the Life Scout award. The big event each year was to spend a week at camp Kootagua in West Va. It was located on the Hughes River about 25 miles from Parkersburg where we used a hand ferry to cross the river. It was a week of tent camping with lots of outdoor experiences.

Another important thing about my school days was that I was an introvert of the introverts. I recall one time when I was in high school a teacher called on me to stand up and read a paragraph. I stood up and read a sentence, and a big grapefruit came up in my throat so that I couldn't say another word. I sat down, humiliated, and said I would never stand up in front of anyone and say anything again. Because of my fear of public speaking, I did not sign up for the public speaking class that was required for graduation. The week before my high school graduation, the principal called me into his office. He wanted to go over my class records. As he looked at the records, he asked why I had not taken the Public Speaking Class, and I told him it was because of my fear of getting up in front of people and saying anything. I did not think he was going to let me graduate from high school, but he made a special dispensation for me, and the night of graduation I received a diploma. That was quite a relief. At that point, little did I know that some day I would be a missionary and speak to large groups of people all around the world.

When I was 14 years old, several of us boys pooled our money and purchased a 1924 Model T Ford car for $50.00. There was only one fellow in the group who was over 16, and had a drivers license. On Sunday afternoons, we would drive it up and down the pasture fields and back roads, and we would be hanging all over the car. Many of the older people in the little town thought we were going to kill ourselves for sure.

The Model T only had two speeds-forward and reverse. It was not gear driven but had bands in the transmission which had to be replaced often; especially when the brakes would wear down, then we would have to tramp the reverse peddle to get it stopped. It did not have a fuel pump, but the gasoline was gravity fed into the carburetor. This meant when we went up a steep hill, we would have to back up the hill in order to get the gas tank high enough to feed the gasoline into the carburetor. We often used bailing wire and tape to keep it going. It was quite an activity for a group of teen age boys.

> *"Make no friendship with an angry man,*
> *And with a furious man do not go,Lest you*
> *learn his ways And set a snare for your soul."*
> Proverbs 22:24-25 NKJV

I'm thankful God used a school administrator to instill in my life this principle.

Life Choices

The day I was 16 years old, I got my automobile driving permit and took my drivers' exam and driving test the same day. Since we lived on a farm I had been driving in the fields for several years. I immediately bought my first car for $50.00. It was a 1929 Model A Ford roadster. It had been sitting in a barn where the chickens had been roosting in it, and the children had been using it as a playhouse. My mother reupholstered it for me, and I discovered shoe polish in the carburetor. After working on the engine for a while and installing a new battery, I got it started, and put some new tires on it. I drove it several thousand miles in the next couple of years and finally sold it for $150.00. I learned a lot about automobiles just working on them during those years.

I loved going to the stock-car races every Saturday night. I had a friend in his late 20's who owned a stock-car and drove it in the races. One Saturday my friend, Tink, and I were at our older friend's garage helping him get his car ready for the races that night. When it was time to go to the races, Tink asked me if I would like to ride with him in his car to the racetrack. He said he would bring me back to the garage when the races were over. I made a quick decision and told him I wanted to ride in the tow truck that pulled the stock-car to the racetrack, and I would meet him there. Then, I would ride back with him in his car after the races. He said, "Okay" and backed his car out into the road to leave. About that time another friend pulled up beside him in his car. They talked to each other briefly, and then their engines revved up, the tires squealed, and they sped down the two-lane road, side-by-side.

I stood in the doorway and watched as they topped the hill, side-by-side, and my friend Tink was on the passing side of the road. I stepped back into the garage and helped the driver hook up the stock-car to the tow truck. Soon we started down the highway in the same direction our friends had gone a few minutes before. I will never forget the sight that I saw as we topped the hill. I had seen Tink and his friend travel side-by-side as they went over the hill, but coming up the other side was a big Mack truck. From the skid marks, it looked like Tink had tried to stop, but he skidded sideways into the front of the big Mack truck; his car bounced off, and went over a ditch through a fence and landed in a creek.

The driver was just climbing out of his truck when we arrived. We asked if he was okay, and then we ran down to where Tink's car had landed. We saw him lying in the car, bleeding and unconscious. There was smoke coming from under the hood, so we decided we better get him out of the car. But when we tried the door was jammed. We ran back up to the tow truck to get some pry bars, and asked some people in a passing car to try to get an ambulance and help. We ran back to Tink's car and pried and pried on the doors until we finally got one door open. We laid him out on the ground just as the ambulance pulled up. The medics ran down and placed him on a stretcher. Just as they placed him in the ambulance I heard him gasping for his last breath. One of my best friends on this Earth was gone out into eternity. I have thought many times about the choice I made in the garage that day, whether I would ride to the racetrack with my friend or in the tow truck. Probably if I had chosen to ride with my friend Tink, I would have gone out into eternity too. For me at that time it would have been a Christ-less eternity. I did not know Christ as my Savior, and it would have meant Hell forever and ever.

"And if it seems evil to you to serve the LORD, choose for yourselves this day whom you will serve, whether the gods which your fathers served that were on the other side of the River, or the gods of the Amorites, in whose land you dwell. But as for me and my house, we will serve the LORD." Joshua 24:15 NKJV

After High School Graduation

In 1952 I graduated from Bartlett High School with 21 in my graduating class. Since I had worked with my dad on the farm during my elementary and high school days he had high hopes that I would become a farmer. He had already given me incentives by letting me have some of my own registered Hereford beef cattle. However, I wanted to leave home and try some new adventures in moneymaking.

Before that was possible, however, the first step was staying at home and working at a company that manufactured mining bolts. This was short-lived, as the job was boring. Soon I was off to a northern Ohio city to work for the Twin Coach Bus Company. There I became a spray painter for new city buses and also buses for the Army, as we were now in the Korean War. I enjoyed seeing the shiny new buses roll off the assembly line. After a couple of years the company had a slowdown, and I was laid off.

At that point several of my friends were going to college, so I enrolled at Ohio State University. I had no idea what I wanted to major in, so classes became a drag, and after one year I dropped out. By this time several of my friends were joining the military for four years, but I decided to wait and let the Army draft me for two years.

It was the day before Christmas when I received a special greeting in the mail. It was from a friend of mine and yours, 'Uncle Sam.' The greeting read like this: "You are selected by your friends and neighbors to serve your country. Report to Fort Hays, Columbus, Ohio on January 21 for a physical exam and induction into the United States Army." On that date some of my friends and I boarded a bus for Fort Hayes, Columbus, Ohio. We took a physical exam, and in a couple of hours they called out my name to line up in the front of the sergeant with a group of other men. He told us we had passed the exam with flying colors, and for us to raise our right hand and repeat with him an oath of allegiance into the United States Army. We did, and we soon found out we were in the Army.

They loaded us onto a Greyhound bus, and we were on our way toward Fort Knox, Kentucky. Once we were there a big, loud sergeant stepped onto the bus and snarled at us to get off the bus and fall in line. We soon found out what he meant as he pointed to a platform with men beside a stack of single mattresses. We were told to "run toward them", and they threw a mattress to each of us. We were told to run with it to a nearby barracks and place it on a cot inside. We did, and soon another sergeant came in with sheets and blankets and told us he was going to teach us how to make our bed. My first thoughts were that my mother had always made my bed, but she wasn't there. My next thought was that making my bed would be easy. But I soon found out that they had an army way for doing every-thing. The sergeant showed us how by taking the sheet and folding it in a certain way, tucking in the corners, and then tightening it up till the bed humped up in the middle. Then he did the blanket the same way. Next he bounced a quarter on the bed, and it sprang up in the air about 6 inches. He then told us to make our beds, and he would come around to inspect them. If the coin didn't bounce 6 inches, he would tear up our bed and make us do it again. I'm not going to tell you how many times I made my bed.

At the beginning of my basic training I was given an M1 rifle and told to keep it with me at all times. That included when we went to the dining hall, when we went out to the drill field, when we went to the classroom, even when we went to bed. I remember that it weighed nine pounds. We had to learn every piece and how it functioned. We had to know how to take it apart and put it back together, as well as how to clean it. In fact, there came a day when they took us to a room, flipped off the lights, and we couldn't see our hand in front of our face. They gave us a limited amount of time to take the gun apart in the dark. Then they flipped on the lights and checked that every part was disassembled. Off went the lights again, and we were told to put it back together in the dark. The ones who didn't have it ready to fire had to keep at this task over and over until they could do it in the allotted time. They told us the reason for this drill was that we may get out on the battlefield some dark night and the gun would jam. Our life and the lives of others might depend on how well we knew our weapon and whether we could take it apart, clean it, and put it back together in the dark. My boot camp training for the infantry was six weeks, and I learned many lessons like these.

The next thing I knew I was assigned to the 510th tank battalion for training on the M-48 tanks. This included driving them, firing the 90 mm gun mounted in the turret, as well as servicing them. It was lots of fun, but the tanks would really get hot inside on extremely hot days. This was during the Korean War, so after the training was completed I expected we would be shipped to Korea. It was not the most comfortable feeling, knowing the enemy had hot phosphorous ammunition that could burn its way right through all of the armor. However, when we received our orders for deployment we were sent to Germany instead of Korea, according to God's sovereign plan. This was one of the greatest things that has ever happened in my life, as you'll learn in the next chapter.

"You therefore must endure hardship as a good soldier of Jesus Christ, No one engaged in warfare entangles himself with the affairs of this life, that he may please him who enlisted him as a soldier. II Timothy 2:3-4 NKJV

Army Days

Just picture a life changing event on board a troop ship with 2600 soldiers, bound for the defeated and war torn country of Germany. An announcement was made over the P.A. system on this hot, July day that only attracted 10 of these G.I.'s to a meeting, where this lone farm boy made a decision that not only affected the course of his life, but left God's foot prints on the lives of several thousand in the years to come. You will read about this amazing story in the pages that follow.

On July 1, 1954 we set sail from Camp Kilmer, New Jersey, to Bremerhaven, Germany. In those days when soldiers were deployed overseas they traveled by ship and not by plane, unless it was an emergency. The ship I was on held 2600 soldiers, and it took approximately 11 days to make the crossing. Since it was summer-time, the weather was warm, and the sailing was smooth.

One day, about halfway across the ocean, an announcement came over the P.A. system that they were having a special Protestant service in one of the lower compartments of the ship. Since it was beautiful outside many of the soldiers were on the deck sunning themselves, and I was lying there half asleep. In fact, I had dozed off when another announcement came over the intercom, **"LAST CALL** for the Protestant service." In the providence of God the loud speaker was right over my head, and it woke me up. At first I thought one would have to be crazy to go down into the stinky, old ship for some religious service on a beautiful day like this. Then I decided to go just to find out who it was that woke me up.

I descended a winding stairwell into the compartment where the service was already in progress. There were 10 men in the room, and a man with a Bible in his hand standing in front of them. I later learned that he was a chaplain on the ship. He was just sharing verses with them and talking to them about how they could be sure of going to heaven when they died. I remember that some of those verses were Romans 3:23, Romans 6:23, Romans 5:8, John 14:6, and John 1:12.

When he finished he said, "If you want to be sure you'll go to heaven when you die, you don't have to take my word for it; just stay behind when I dismiss the meeting, and I will show you in the Bible how you can be sure." Then he dismissed the meeting, and everyone left except me. He came back to where I was seated and asked if I was interested in going to heaven when I died. I told him I was. He asked if I was a sinner. I told him I was sure I was. He asked me if I believed the Bible, and I told him I had no reason to doubt it. Then he asked me to read some of the verses he had quoted and given in his talk. As I read them he asked me if I understood them, and when not, he explained them. Then he asked me if I was willing to admit to Jesus that I was a sinner and ask Him to save me. At that point I told him I had never prayed and didn't know how. He told me I could talk to Jesus just like I was talking to him. He said that he could even pray a sinner's prayer, and I could repeat the words after him. The key was that I was meaning in my heart what the words were saying. He then prayed phrase by phrase, and I repeated after him; and I did mean it in my heart. After we prayed, he showed me I John 5:14 and 15, which explains how God heard my prayer and gave me what I asked for, which was salvation.

I had a praying mother who was concerned about my going overseas without knowing the Lord. I really believe that everything that took place on the ship that day was in answer to her prayers. Just think of the odds of me accepting Christ at this time. There were 2600 soldiers on the ship; only 10 went to this meeting, and only one trusted Christ, and that was me. Thank God for His sovereign grace.

Soon after that meeting I wrote a letter to my mother and told her that I had trusted Christ as my Savior. After she went home to be with the Lord, we found that letter in her keepsakes, and here is an excerpt from it..

Dearest Mother, Sun Aug 8th

> *"What I have got to say is what I know you have wanted to hear me say for years. I am so happy and know you will be overjoyed too, that I've taken the Lord into my heart as my personal saviour. Now I can see for myself what you've tried to tell me mother dear. It was actually on the boat coming across the Atlantic where I saw the light when a Chaplain spoke to me." Your loving son Louis*

We arrived in Germany early Sunday morning and traveled by train that day from Bremerhaven to Mannheim where I was stationed at Sullivan Barracks for the next 19 months. Since we arrived late Sunday afternoon, I decided I would start out my new Christian life by going to church. I found out there was a chapel near my barracks, so I walked there, only to find out it was dark. I walked on to find out if there was an evening service any place on the base, and to my disappointment, there didn't seem to be a service any place.

On my way back I passed the dark chapel again, but noticed a light in one of the rooms on the second floor. I

30

decided to try the door, and it was unlocked. I stepped inside and could hear some voices, so I went up the stairway to the second floor. There were four young men having a Bible study in one of the rooms, and they heard me on the stairs and came to greet me. They invited me to the Bible study and asked me to share my testimony. They were excited to hear that I had just been saved on the ship. They told me they had permission to use this room in the chapel each Sunday night for the Bible study, and invited me to come. I started attending every week, and began to grow in the Lord.

The group began expanding in attendance, and when I left there 19 months later, we had grown to about 200 and were given permission to meet in the main chapel. They had many activities going on each week, and eventually I was asked to teach a young boys' Sunday school class. It was a wonderful place to grow in my new-found faith, and most of my off-duty time revolved around this group.

Since we were serving as an occupation army in Germany after the Second World War, I was spending my early days out on the tank line doing maintenance. This work involved taking bolts off and putting them back on day after day, which became very boring. I had become acquainted with the Battalion supply clerk, and he asked if I could type. I told him I had taken a typing class when I was in high school, but had never used it. He told me he was soon rotating back to the States, so possibly I could get his job. With the winter approaching, and the weather getting cold, this appealed to me. So he introduced me to his boss, who was the captain of the Battalion.

To make a long story short, I was given his job which involved lots of typing, as I was responsible for ordering all the supplies for the Battalion. This job kept me out of the cold weather, out of guard duty, KP, and a whole host of other things. This was great, but little did I realize how valuable this typing practice would be to me in my ministry for the Lord in the years ahead.

As my days in the Army drew to a close, there was lots of pressure to re-enlist, but I knew that a career in the Army was not for me. On December 24 1955, I was shipped back to the States, and in January 1956 I was discharged and on my way to live with my parents in Ohio.

> *The Lord is not slack concerning His promise, as some count slackness, but is longsuffering toward us, not willing that any should perish but that all should come to repentance."* II Peter 3:9 NKJV

First Missionary Journey

When I arrived back home from the Army, my mother was attending a new church. She had been a Sunday school teacher in the church we attended when I was growing up. She liked teaching, but found some issues with the material the church supplied for her to use. She told the Sunday school superintendent that she didn't agree with some of the material and would just like to use her Bible to teach from in the class. He told her that if she didn't agree with the material she should find herself another church.

There was a new church starting about 6 miles away, so she started attending there. On my first weekend back from the Army she invited me to go with her. The first Sunday I was there the pastor said from the pulpit, they had been praying for someone to work with the teens in the church, and God had answered their prayers. He announced that I was back from the service, and that I would be their new teen youth director. He hadn't said anything to me about it, so I cornered him at the door and asked him why he had said I was the new youth director. He sort of laughed and said I could do it. He had already ordered the materials, and they would soon arrive in a box and would be easy to follow. I reluctantly agreed to try it. I was a rather new Christian and did not know much about my Bible. I liked working with the young people, but struggled with teaching the material.

I got a job with E.I. DuPont, working first in the mail room and later in the storeroom. I also purchased a dump truck and hired a driver to haul gravel for the roads during the week, and on the weekends I would put a large tank on the dump bed and haul water for farmers. There was an offset printing press in the DuPont mail room. Between my mail runs around the plant on a motor scooter, I would often help the person running the printing press and learned how to operate it. A few times he didn't show up, and I would run off some things for them. Little did I know how God was training me for the future.

After about two years of this work routine and leading the teens at church, I felt restless. I didn't want to spend the rest of my life in this type of work, and I felt I needed some Bible training to minister to the teens. In the spring of 1958 I decided to resign my job, sell my truck, and take a trip to southern Mexico to visit my brother who was a director of the jungle training camp for Wycliffe Bible translators. Soon I found myself driving in my new Mercury hardtop to Mexico City, and then on to Chiapas, approximately 750 miles south of there.

About halfway on my trip I stopped in a small village to spend the night. The place where I stayed was pretty rustic, and the room they gave me faced the street right outside my window. There was so much drinking and loud talking outside of my window I couldn't sleep. In the middle of the night I got up, got dressed, and went to my car and headed south.

It was dark, and much of the highway had high mountains on each side. It had rained continuously and many rocks were coming down on the road. A little after daylight, I was following a car that was swerving back and forth across the highway in front of me in order to dodge the rocks. I thought if this car missed the rocks it would be safe for me to pass. What I didn't realize was that his car was higher than mine. All at once there was a big bang under my car, and my muffler started making a loud noise and a hissing sound. I realized that one of the big rocks I had tried to straddle had hit my tailpipe and muffler.

I knew I needed to do something, so I started to look for a place to get my car fixed. I found an outdoor garage in someone's yard, so I stopped. My problem was that I could not speak the Spanish language. So I motioned to the mechanic to come, and pointed up under my car. He looked under it, shook his head, and got a jack and tools to start working on it. He had to cut and weld some things, but soon I was on my way. Praise the Lord for His provision.

I went as far as the road would take me at that time to a place called Xtapa, which was a flight base for Missionary Aviation Fellowship to fly missionaries into the remote areas. On this last stretch of road it was dark, and I was winding up a hill when a man stepped out in front of me, waving his hands for me to stop. Since I didn't know what his motives were I didn't know what to do. I decided to keep going, hoping he would get out of the way. But when he didn't move, I swerved at the last minute to miss him and go on. I guess I never will know if he had some harm planned for me, or if he just wanted a ride, or needed some help.

I parked my car at the MAF base and stayed overnight with the pilot. The next morning we flew in a Cessna 180 plane about 100 miles over mountainous terrain to Wycliffe's jungle training camp. I had talked with my brother about coming, but he did not know the exact time. When we landed in a pasture field beside the missionary training station my brother Wayne, his wife Arlene, and their three boys David, Dennis, and Donnie, came out to the plane thinking supplies had arrived. My arrival was a big surprise when I got off the plane. They were very excited and happy to see me.

This was a new experience for me to live in a mud hut with a grass roof and a mud floor. Some of their camp residents were missionaries, but others were Celtal Indians who spoke a language I had never heard before, and dressed in a much different way than I had ever seen before. I spent the entire summer at this location, and sometimes flew with MAF to visit other Indian tribes and missionaries in the area of Mexico, just north of the Guatemalan border.

I spent the entire summer helping in any way I could at jungle camp and at the various Indian tribes with Wycliffe translators. I remember one time hiking over a muddy trail through the forest for about an hour to a Celtal village where Wycliffe missionaries had translated the Bible into their language. I remember coming into the village of mud huts along with one larger building that had been white washed. When I asked what it was, they told me it was their church. Almost the entire tribe in that village had trusted Christ as Savior.

There was a stream of water that ran through the village, and the missionary had made an electric turbine, powered by the flow of water, that generated electric lights for the church. That night they had a service, and they asked me to give my testimony. As we went into the service I noticed benches outside the windows. I asked what these were. They explained to me that people who had committed sin against others in the church had to sit outside and were not allowed to come inside during the services. They had to do that until they had asked forgiveness from the Lord and made a public confession before the people. Then they would be welcomed back inside the church. I was very surprised to see several people sitting on the benches, looking in that night, as I gave my testimony. How many people in America do you think would do that?

One Sunday afternoon at jungle camp a man from a nearby village came running to see my brother. He said there was a lady in the village who was in her hut screaming and beating herself, and he wanted my brother to come and see if he could do anything. My brother turned to me and said, "Let's go with him." We hiked up the mountainside to where the lady was lying in her mud hut. This woman was still screaming, shaking all over and beating herself. All of us went inside, and immediately my brother began to pray and command the demon inside of her to come out in the name of Jesus Christ. Soon she stopped screaming, shaking, and beating herself. I had never seen anything like this before, and never have since. On our walk back to jungle camp, my brother told me that there were people in the tribes who were demon possessed and from time to time would do very strange things. Prayer in Jesus' name was the only thing that would drive the demons out.

> *"I can do all things through Christ who strengthens me."* Phil 4:13

Farm Boy Meets Farm Girl

While I was in Mexico, I began to think about where I should go for Bible training. I began thumbing through some Moody Monthly magazines that my brother had, and looked at the advertisements for a Bible Institute, a Bible college, or a Christian liberal arts college. As I looked through the ads, I ran across one that pictured several pretty girls, and thought that it looked like a good place for me to go. It was Philadelphia College of the Bible (later Philadelphia Biblical University). So I sent for an application and mailed it in.

When I arrived back at my home in the United States in late August I had received a letter of acceptance and the school term was to start in just a few days. Philadelphia Bible Institute and Philadelphia School of the Bible had merged into Philadelphia Bible College. Charles Ryrie was the new president. He was around 30 years of age, still single, with three earned Doctorate degrees.

I still remember the first day I was there. Dr. Ryrie arrived in his bright, shiny convertible to take the reins of the school. He became a favorite teacher, and we all looked forward to his chapel messages each Friday. These messages later became a book called <u>Let's Talk Turkey</u>. Several years after that the name was changed to <u>Patterns for Christian Living</u>.

The first few nights this farm boy didn't sleep much in the center of the big city of Philadelphia on the eighth floor of Philadelphia College of the Bible. Every time a police or fire sound went off I would jump out of bed and run to the fire escape, which was not far from my bedroom door. I was sure the building was on fire. However, it wasn't many nights until I didn't even hear these alarms.

All I did the first couple of months in college was go to class and study. However, I needed money to stay in school and was able to get a job at National Car Rental, just one block from the school. I went to school in the morning, ate lunch, and worked from one o'clock to six o'clock every afternoon. I felt that God provided this job for me, and I was able to keep it for the next four years. I also was able to park my car free at work, as parking anywhere else in downtown Philadelphia was very expensive.

Every morning before class I attended the homeland prayer group. One reason I went to the homeland group was because of my interest in some type of youth ministry in the United States. One ministry I learned about and we prayed for was the starting of a new Bible camp in southern Illinois called the Duckels' Bible camp, where a farmer was in the process of turning part of his farm into a camp. His oldest daughter, Thelma, was a student at Philadelphia College of the Bible. She came to PCB to take Bible courses, as she was already a graduate of a Christian liberal arts college. She came faithfully to the prayer meeting each morning. Sometimes we prayed together, and this was the way I got to know her and learn what her interests were.

Several months passed before I asked her for a date. Our first date was to a basketball game, when Philadelphia College of the Bible played Nyack Missionary College on their court. We liked each other, but it was not a serious relationship. Besides, once when she was in high school she had told her father that she would never marry a farmer. When the school year was over, she planned to go back to her home in Illinois, and I planned to stay in Philadelphia to work at National Car Rental for the summer.

Thelma made arrangements to ride back to Illinois with a couple of girls, but they couldn't go until 10 days after classes ended. During these 10 days she needed a chaperone for supper, so we ate together each evening. As a result we got to know each other much better. But when she left we didn't know if we would ever see each other again.

During that summer, National Car Rental asked me to drive a leased car to St. Louis. From there I was to pick up another car and drive it to Grand Rapids. This route went by the Duckels' Bible Camp (her home) on the way. I then was to pick up another car in Michigan and drive it back to Philadelphia. My boss told me I could take a few days along the way to visit if I wanted to do so. I called Thelma and asked if it would be okay if I stopped by the Duckels' Bible camp and visit her. She agreed, I met her parents, and we decided to keep in touch.

Soon she applied and was accepted to be a missionary with Bible Club Movement Incorporated and came back to Camp Sankanac near Philadelphia for training. I was still enrolled at Philadelphia College of the Bible for the next three years, so we saw each other several times during her training. She was assigned as a missionary to teach in the public schools in the Corning, New York area.

During that next year our relationship grew more serious as we traveled back and forth between Philadelphia and Corning several times. I still had two more years to complete at Philadelphia College of the Bible and the college had a rule that you could not get married during your college days without their permission. Since I was older than most students and had already been in the army, I asked for permission, and they granted it. I bought a ring, and during Christmas vacation, we drove to my parents in Ohio for a few days so she could meet them. Then we drove on to Illinois, to her parents' home, for Christmas. While there I asked her to marry me, and she accepted. We then planned our wedding for the following June, to be held in the brand-new chapel at her parents' camp.

The date was set for Sunday afternoon on June 12, 1960. I arrived at the Duckels Bible Camp a few days before the wedding, and stayed in one of the boys cabins on the campground. I spent several days on the lawnmower helping spruce things up for the big event. Thelma's dad and a local pastor performed the ceremony in the new camp chapel. Thelma's sister, Faye, and her roommate from college took part in the wedding. Two of my friends drove from Ohio to be in our wedding and one was able to bring my mother. It was a happy day, with a reception following at the camp dining hall. Immediately that afternoon, we started driving south.

I planned to take Thelma to meet my brother and his family, in Mexico, and then spend our honeymoon at Jungle Camp, along with visiting other missionaries for the next two months, before returning to Philadelphia College of Bible in the fall. On the way, we stopped at Veracruz, Mexico for a couple of days of sightseeing. I became deathly sick from some food and my bride thought she was going to be a widow within a few days of our wedding. She found an air-conditioned hotel and met a woman whose husband had also been sick. She told Thelma they had seen a doctor who prescribed some pills for her husband. He only took one pill and was fine. She asked Thelma if she would like one of these pills for me. Thelma came back to the room and told me about meeting this woman and asked if I wanted to chance one of these pills. I was so sick I said, "Bring it; I'm going to die anyway." I took it, and the next day I was well enough to drive over 600 Miles.

We flew in the same plane I had taken two years earlier into the Wycliffe Training Camp. They had a little mud hut all ready for us with a wedding bell hanging over the bed. The first night I looked up in the rafters and saw where a snake had shed its skin, but I didn't tell Thelma.

This was our home for two months, except for a side trip to the Lockendon Indian tribe where Phil and Mary Bear were trying to translate the Scriptures. At that time, they had been there for 14 years without one convert. The Indians would trick them when they would ask what a certain thing was by giving them the wrong name. This greatly slowed down the translation process.

The men had more than one wife, and when the men would go to the fields to work during the day the women would get into big fights and pull each others hair out. At one point, the Indians all moved many miles away to a new location and left the missionaries by themselves. The missionaries loved these people so much that they followed them and built a new house, where they lived when we arrived.

We stayed behind their house in a bamboo pole hut which had big cracks in the walls. We slept inside in hammocks stretched between poles. When we went to bed, there would be Indians peeking through the cracks, and when we got up, there would be eyes peeking through the same cracks. They watched us almost every minute. They noticed that Thelma had two rings on her finger (engagement ring and wedding band) and asked if she would give them one of the rings.

We took a softball and bat along and taught them how to play ball. They would strike at the ball and miss, and then just lie down and laugh. When they hit the ball, they would laugh so hard they couldn't run. It was fun teaching them this game and spending time with them.

It was a very hot climate there. At night it would cool down to around 100°F. The only way you could cool off was to lie down in a mountain stream. Another missionary brought in a gasoline generator, and I helped him hook up to some lights. While I was there, the Indians wanted us to string some wires out to their cornfields so they could work at night when it was cooler.

Each Indian family had a god house behind their regular house. They would form a god pot out of clay which had an ugly face on it, and place it in the god house. Then they would burn pine tar in the pot. While this was happening they would soak some kind of weed in a vat with water, and drink the juice from it. It would make them drunk, and they would dance around this god pot in a drunken stupor, repeating a chant. This shows how every person is made to worship something.

> *"But seek first the kingdom of God and His righteousness, and all these things shall be added to you."* Matthew. 6:33 NKJV

Steps of Faith in the Ministry

During most of my days at Philadelphia College of the Bible, I was the youth director at Immanuel Baptist Church in Maple Shade, New Jersey. Herbert Mitchell was the pastor of that great church during those days, and I learned many leadership principles and skills under his leadership. Also, this was the first church to support us as a missionary family, and they have continued to support us for over 50 years.

I remember that soon after I started leading the teens in that church, Pastor Mitchell called me into his office and gave me a calendar. He asked me what my lesson was for the next Sunday. I told him I usually didn't know what my topic would be for Sunday until the Saturday night before I was going to teach the next day.

He told me he would like me to decide what my lessons would be for the next eight weeks and put them on the calendar. Then he wanted me to plan some kind of group Christian service every week for the next eight weeks and to put that on the calendar, (a tract blitz, rest home service, ministry at the local rescue mission, etc.). Then he wanted me to plan some type of social activity once a month and to put that on my calendar. He asked me to bring my calendar for him to see within the next week, because he would put everything on the church calendar. He said, "If you aim at nothing, you'll be sure to hit it every time." That is just one of many lessons he taught me while I was there, and it has been invaluable to me over the years.

When I began my final year at Philadelphia College of the Bible, I still didn't know for sure what the Lord wanted me to do, but I did think the Lord wanted me to be involved in some type of youth ministry. One day we had a chapel speaker, named Paul Bubar, who was the new Bible club director from Word of Life. He told us about a new Bible club program for teens that Word of Life was starting. He explained that the clubs would be church centered, church sponsored, and led by laymen in the churches. He went on to tell us that Word of Life would supply the material, train the laymen how to use it, and continue to work with the church in activities to reach the unsaved teens of their area, and help disciple them and channel them into their church.

This really sounded exciting to me and something of which I would like to be a part. So I asked Paul if I could talk to him about it as soon as the chapel was over. We met in the Snack Shack, and he told me that this was a new program for Word of Life, and that they would need staff to spread out across the United States and coordinate these clubs. I told him my wife and I would definitely like to be a part of it. He asked some questions about my background, took down my name, address, and phone number, and said he would get in touch with me. I waited and waited, but heard nothing.

A few weeks later, Jack Wyrtzen, the founder and director of Word of Life, came to Philadelphia for a rally (evangelistic meeting). Thelma and I attended the meeting, and when it was over, Jack announced that he would be down front to talk to anyone who would like to talk to him. People lined up, and we got in line.

When we got up to him, we exchanged a few words of greeting, and then I said, "What is wrong with that fellow you have in charge of your Bible club program?" It was evident that Jack was startled some what by my question and wanted to know if I was referring to Paul Bubar, and why I was asking him this question. I told him that I was very interested in being a part of the Word of Life Bible Club ministry, but Paul would not answer my letters. Jack took down my name, but then changed the subject and didn't say anything about Paul.

However, the next day I got a phone call from Paul, and he arranged for us to come to the home office in Orange, New Jersey and talk with him. I found out later that he was looking for someone with an outgoing personality, and he didn't really think that I had what was needed and sort of hoped I would go away.

That meeting in Orange was the beginning of a lifelong friendship, and Paul has been not only my boss for over 40 years, but my closest friend. His style of leadership not only allowed me to grow and mature spiritually, but also gave me the opportunity to see the Lord do things in and through my life that I never dreamed would be possible. I can never thank Paul enough for being such a great boss and a great friend all of these years.

Soon after my graduation from PCB, in June 1962, our first son Steve was born. Six weeks later, we were invited to go to Word of Life Island. We walked up "Cardiac Hill" and into Jack Wyrtzen's office. Jack shook hands with us and said, "Welcome to the family of Word of Life, take good care of that little boy, and go get'em." That was our policy school and induction into Word of Life, all in one ceremony.

You need to realize that at that point Word of Life was a very small organization. Soon after being in the ministry, I remember being in a meeting of our entire staff worldwide, and we all sat around one large table in our home office in New Jersey. After camp was over in Schroon Lake each summer, everything was closed down for the winter, and the full-time staff went back to New Jersey.

We were asked to raise our support, and in a couple of months we had $100 raised. At that time, there was no rule in Word of Life about how much money we had to raise before going to our field. We were in the process of taking our big step of living by faith, and only a few days before resigning my job at National Car Rental, when I received a letter from a well known Youth Organization in Cincinnati, Ohio. They had heard that I graduated from college and was thinking about youth ministry. They asked me to consider a position with them that included a good monthly salary, a housing allowance, and a car to drive. It could have been a temptation, but we were so sure that God was calling us to Word of Life; we didn't consider it.

We decided to move right away to where we were assigned to pioneer the Word of Life Bible Club ministry. We had a Volkswagen bug, and I was able to buy a truck from National Car Rental where I worked. The truck had not been running for several months and was sitting on the back side of the lot. I asked the mechanic about it, and he said all it needed was a new timing chain and that he would help me put it on some Saturday. I offered the boss $50 for the truck and he took it. It had a large enclosed bed and a power lift gate. With the new timing chain, it ran fine, and we moved all our belongings from New Jersey to Ohio.

A lady, whom my mother had led to the Lord, heard we were going to be missionaries and offered us her house, completely furnished, to live in rent-free. It was a farmhouse out in the country in southeastern Ohio. She was living in California and wanted us to try to sell it for her while we lived there.

Since we only had $100 a month coming in, we didn't have much for food, utilities, clothing, gasoline, and etc. Churches had food showers for us; club leaders who lived on farms and had large gas tanks for their tractors began to put gas in our car. Another farmer called and told us he had butchered our beef. When we told him we didn't have any beef, he said one of the cows in the field had our name on it,

47

and he had butchered it and had it cut and wrapped for us. About six months later, he called and said he'd butchered our pork, and it was the same as the beef. He kept doing this for us for several years.

A dentist friend who had a boy about a year or two older than our Steve sent us his clothes as he outgrew them. We found out we didn't need much money when the Lord met all our needs through churches and other Christians. This continued when we didn't have much support, but as we gained support and could buy our own things these provisions through others began to diminish. We found out that His promise to meet "all of our needs according to His riches in glory by Christ Jesus" was true. What an exciting way to live!

One day I was coming down the highway in our little green Volkswagen bug, when suddenly there was a big bang and the engine died. I coasted over to the side of the road, got out and looked under the car, there was a big pool of oil dripping from the engine. I called a tow truck to take it to a nearby garage and the mechanic said it would cost $300 to fix it. I thumbed home, and when I came walking in Thelma asked me what had happened and why I looked so sad. I explained that we had no money to fix the car, and that was our only means of transportation. About that time the phone rang. It was Paul Bubar, my boss, calling. He asked how things were going. When I told him about the car, he asked if I was sitting down or standing up. I told him I was standing by the wall phone, and he said, "You better sit down. The reason I called was to tell you that we just received a check from a businessman in Cleveland, Ohio for $300, and it was designated for Lou Nicholes' car." It was the exact amount I needed to repair the car, and the check had been written before the car broke down! That was the first time this man had ever given anything toward our ministry, and he never gave anything after that. It was only our great God taking care of us.

"And my God shall supply all your need according to His riches in glory by Christ Jesus." Philippians 4:19 NKJV

Bible Club Years

Our 26 years with the Word of Life Bible Club ministry were challenging, exciting, and very fruitful. When we started my vision was to help local churches in the Ohio Valley with their youth. This consisted basically of southeastern Ohio and part of West Virginia. I really had no idea of all God was going to do, and how He would stretch me in the process. One of the things I am very thankful for is that my leadership was not threatened, and allowed me to use my God given talents and abilities to help develop the material, methods, and programs for the new Word of Life Clubs.

Our years with Word of Life can basically be divided into three areas of ministry:

1. Twenty-six years in Word of Life Bible Clubs.

2. Twelve years in short-term missions called Youth Reach-out.

3. Twelve plus years as the Asia representative for Word of Life.

In this chapter you will learn about some of my experiences in the Word of Life Bible Club ministry. In 1962, Thelma and I, with our son Steve, moved to Marietta, Ohio to pioneer the Bible Club ministry, and to represent Word of Life in the Midwest.

Up to this time Word of Life was known mostly on the east coast of the U.S.; so in a farmer's terminology, you could say, I was "plowing new ground." Most people in this area of the country had never heard of Jack Wyrtzen or Word of Life. In order to sell the program to local churches, I needed to know the program; so I decided to convince a local church in the area to sponsor a club. I offered to lead the club myself and got other layman in the church to help me. That way I was not trying to teach other people how to do things I was not doing myself.

I suggested that we meet on Saturday night in a neutral location so we could draw young people who were not regular attendees at the church. I purchased a burned-out mobile home and fixed it up as a clubhouse and my office, and we parked it in our yard. Between 20 and 30 teens began coming every Saturday night to our club. We also started other teen clubs in other churches in the Ohio and West Va. area.

Since the Word of Life Club ministry was new, we were trying to develop new materials and programs as we went along. Things that succeeded for us we tried with the other new clubs we were starting. Paul Bubar was writing the Bible studies and mimeographing them and sending them to us.

One day a gentleman gave me an offset printing press to print my prayer letters and other materials. I had learned how to operate a press when I worked for E. I. DuPont, so I was glad to have it. Soon Paul Bubar saw some of my printed things and compared it to his mimeographed things and asked if I could print the Bible studies instead of using mimeographing material. Of course, I said, "Yes," because we were only doing a few hundred for everyone at that time. However, as the club ministry grew across the United States we began to print more Bible studies and other materials, and I needed more help.

By this time Word of Life had added more Bible Club men in other states. John Venlet, Dick Johnson, and Bob

Anderson agreed to come and help me print and bind the Bible studies. The next year while they were there we were talking about the need for a reading outline for our Quiet-Time. Up to this point we just printed pages for a very small notebook that only asked two questions, "What is the writer saying?", and "How can I apply this to my life?" ,and no verses were suggested for daily reading.

After a while, we saw how many teens just picked some of the same passages over and over and never read much of the Bible. So while we were doing the Bible studies, we talked about how great it would be to add a reading outline for the whole Bible and bind these into booklets for each year. We then wondered what to call it, and one person (I think Dick Johnson) suggested we call it a "Quiet Time Diary." We were all excited about this, so I called Paul Bubar and told him about our idea. He listened and then said, "It sounds like a good idea, but I don't think it will work." When I asked why, he said, "A diary is a girl thing and I don't think boys will go for it." I then asked if we could try it in a couple of areas, and he said, "Sure, go for it."

I volunteered to work on the outlines for reading, and we agreed to try to cover the whole Bible in six years. I worked on the outlines for two years but became busy with too many other things so John Venlet took it over for many years. This "Quiet Time Diary" soon became popular and swept the country. Now it is printed in many languages around the world. It started out as teen material, but soon many adults wanted to use it, and eventually this was adapted for various age groups of children.

As the Bible Club program grew, we needed more and more materials, and I needed a secretary. We hired Bernice Wagner, both as my secretary and printer, and she stayed with us for 22 years. Her husband Chuck was a club leader, and her girls were very active in the Club program which was a great asset to the ministry.

Our boys, Steve and Mike, started working in the print shop at a very early age after school and on Saturdays. We continued to print the Quiet Time Diary until we reached 40,000 copies per year, and our boys graduated from high school. Then we had to give the job to others. Many people have said the Quiet Time Diary is the greatest tool Word of Life has ever produced.

I worked alone in the Bible club program in the Midwest area for about eight years as the Bible clubs expanded. I reached a total of about 60 clubs, but that was all I could service. We advertised that we didn't just send material, but we came along in the box and jumped out to help. I would try to meet in small groups with every leader for leadership training classes every six weeks and visit their clubs as often as possible.

Finally, Paul Bubar said that in order to grow the club program, we needed to start adding staff in my region; and he would make me a Regional Director to train and coordinate the staff. I loved working with the layman and teens in the churches, and I didn't want to give up that relationship, so I rebelled in my heart for almost a year. I was miserable. I told Thelma I couldn't go on like that. She suggested that we pray about it; so one afternoon we got down on our knees in our living room and prayed most of the afternoon. When I got up I said, "Okay God, I will do what my boss wants me to do and be a Regional Director."

At that point our club count began to go up, and our ministry began to grow. We saw the need for a leadership conference to launch the new club year; so we held the first one at the 4-H Club Campground in Ripley, West Va. with 16 in attendance. This developed into an annual two day leadership conference for the entire region that we called a "Blueprint for Leadership", and it grew to between 700-800 in attendance each year. For many years, it was held the first weekend in September on the Cedarville College campus in Cedarville, Ohio.

We would dispense all of the new club materials for the year and hold seminars for the leaders. We always had special music and invited well-known motivational speakers from across the country such as, Warren Wiersbe, Jerry Farwell, Lee Robertson, Charles Tremendous Jones, Jack Wyrtzen, and Harry Bollback. It was always a highlight of the year. In the middle of the year each of our staff men would hold a small one day area wide conference for their leaders to encourage them; and, usually, I would go to help them. At the peak of my time in the club ministry, I had nine men ministering with me in Ohio, West Virginia, Indiana, and Michigan. Not because of me, but because of God's grace and His blessing, we had 262 Bible clubs when I left that region to start Youth Reachout in 1988.

Another highlight of the year for our family was the annual Club Conference held in Schroon Lake, New York, for our Club staff. It was usually in December and the only time each year all of our Bible Club staff across the nation would come together. We would always be introduced to new materials, be challenged by our leaders, Jack, Harry, George, Paul, and others, as well as learn new leadership techniques. There were always special times for the ladies, as well as the men, and lots of time for sharing and bonding as a Word of Life family. We always chose to bring our children with us, even though the program was not necessarily geared for them, because we always wanted them to feel a part of our ministry and get to know all of our wonderful leaders. I believe this is a major reason all three of our children (Steve, Mike and Beth) are missionaries with Word of Life today in Asia.

> *"I know your works. See, I have set before you an open door, and no one can shut it, for you have a little strength, have kept My word, and have not denied My name."* Revelation 3:8 NKJV

Does God Really Answer Prayer?

For 26 years we were very much involved in the Word of Life Bible Club ministry in what is often referred to as the Midwest part of the United States. This included the states of Ohio, West Virginia, Indiana, and Michigan.

As the Regional Director for Word of Life, I crisscrossed these states often, ministering in local churches and helping them with their youth programs. I often jokingly said that I traveled the same roads so much that I knew every crack in the road and every good restaurant in the area.

During the mid 1970's, someone purchased and gave us a 27 foot travel trailer which we used in the summer, traveling from church to church. Let me tell you a story about answered prayer.

One day we were traveling from Michigan back to our home in Ohio, pulling the trailer with our Chevy Suburban. We were going down an interstate highway in Indiana when I heard a strange sound. I pulled over to the side of the road, got out and went back to see what the problem was. It was a safety chain on the tongue of the travel trailer. I stooped over and picked the chain up, which was banging on the highway, and I hooked it to the vehicle. Then I got back in the vehicle and traveled on down the road. We arrived home that night.

We had been gone for several days, and so we had a pile of mail that had collected while we were gone. I opened the mail, and there were several bills to pay. I looked for my checkbook, but I couldn't find it. We made a big search of the house and the things that we had taken with us on our trip, but there was no checkbook. I had to leave the next day to go on another trip, so I told Thelma we would pray and trust God to show us the checkbook so we could pay our bills.

We prayed and asked God to help us find the checkbook, but it didn't turn up that day or before I had to leave on the trip. I called back a day or two later to see if the checkbook had shown up. Then Thelma told me a letter had come in the mail from Indiana. A lady had written from Ashley, Indiana and said she and her granddaughter were riding down the interstate in their car when they noticed something blowing along the highway. The granddaughter said, "Grandma, Grandma, stop and see what that is." So, the lady said, "We pulled over to the side of the highway and went back and found your checkbook. It had your name, your address, and your phone number. I tried calling you, but there was no answer; so I'm writing to ask you, what I should do with the checkbook?" She said, "Would you want to pick it up, or have me send it to you?" Then she signed the letter, 'In Christ'. This was not an accident. I believe that God sent this lady and her granddaughter along the highway, and they pulled over and found our checkbook. Normally, someone would not stop if they just saw something as small as this along the highway.

Once when we were on a Youth Reachout trip to Asia, we stopped on our way in Hawaii to do a weekend ministry. It was Sunday, and we had a terrific ministry in two different churches. Our group, of 75, was scheduled to fly out of Honolulu at 12:30 a.m., Monday morning, to continue our missions trip. We had arranged with the bus company to pick us up at 9:00 p.m. where we were staying and take us to the airport. The time came, and all of our young people were excited and ready to go; but the buses didn't arrive.

After waiting awhile, we became concerned and tried to call the bus company; but all we could get was an answering machine because it was Sunday, and no one was on duty. We got all the young people together and asked them to pray. A couple of us got on phones and started calling everyone we thought could help. We knew it was a serious problem because if we missed our flight with 75 people, it would be very difficult to reschedule anytime soon and would cost lots of money. I called the airport to tell them our problem and asked if they knew how we might reach someone at the bus company. They gave me a dispatcher number, and I tried it; but there was no answer.

Everyone was praying. In a few minutes I tried again, and this time a driver who had just arrived back from his bus run heard the phone and answered it. Normally, he would have just hung up his keys and left for the day. When I told him our problem, he checked the log and saw that they were planning to pick us up Monday instead of Sunday evening. He yelled to another driver just back from another run. Then he said, "We will be right there to pick you up." They came and we barely made our flight, but the airlines did everything they could to rush us through customs, security, and check-in procedures. It was a miracle that we got the dispatcher number, that the bus driver answered the phone, that the 2nd driver just "happened" to be there, and that the airlines helped us make our flight. All of us knew that God had answered our prayers.

> *"Now this is the confidence that we have in Him, that if we ask anything according to His will, He hears us. And if we know that He hears us, whatever we ask, we know that we have the petitions that we have asked of Him."* I John 5:14-15 NKJV

Evangelistic Events

Anyone who knows much about Word of Life knows it is centered in evangelism and discipleship. In my 26 years in Word of Life Bible clubs, I was involved in thousands of exciting evangelistic events. This consisted of everything from Jack Wyrtzen rallies to Operation Nightmares.

We simply used good fun and laughter to get the ear of all ages, and then we preached the gospel to them. I cannot possibly begin to tell you about all of these events in which I was involved; but in those wonderful years, we saw over 40,000 people make a decision for Christ, and our counselors were privileged to counsel them. Then we always tried to channel these new converts into a local Bible believing church.

Some of these events were all-day Basketball Marathons with as many as 100 ball teams playing in one city in one day, using many college and high school gyms. At the end of the day we gave away beautiful trophies to the players on the winning teams.

At one of these marathons on a Saturday in Dayton, Ohio, we had the schedule posted and the games underway. I was just breathing a sigh of relief when the janitor of the school came to tell me I had a phone call. Our speaker that day was to be George Theis, a Word of Life missionary to Brazil, who was in the United States on furlough. When I got to the phone, he explained that his car had broken down, and he was several hours away and would not be able to make the meeting in time to speak during the noon time break.

My heart sank. I had organized many events in the past eight years, but never before had experienced a speaker not showing up. I mentioned earlier when I was in high school I was the introvert of the introverts and afraid to get up and speak before a crowd. I didn't even take a public speaking class because of this fear. I felt that my gift was organization, not preaching.

Don Kinzer had just arrived as a new Bible Club Representative in my region, and I was training him. I told him the speaker was not coming, because his car had broken down, and I didn't know what to do. He looked at me and said, "I don't know much about running a Basketball Marathon, but I will do my best, and I think you better get ready to speak."

I took my Bible and went back to the furnace room and begged God for a message. When the time came, I spoke that day with much fear and trembling. I had watched many speakers give invitations, so I tried to remember how they had done it, and when I gave the invitation to trust Christ, I thought I had done a miserable job. No one could have been more surprised than I was when over 30 came forward to be counseled for salvation. It just showed me how God can use anyone if he is willing. This was the beginning of God using me to speak at many events all over the world in coming years.

We sponsored Volleyball Marathons in many areas with hundreds of young people coming to know Christ. Eventually we added Softball Marathons, and a regional playoff at Bowling Green University each year. One end of the stadium was packed with players and spectators for the preaching of the gospel at noontime.

Another exciting event was fun night, which we called a 'Thingamajig' which consisted of a lot of crazy games and competition. Don "Robbie" Robertson was one of our favorite speakers for these events. One night I was with Jim Neahusan in Flint, Michigan for one of these, and I was the speaker. Over 1000 young people attended that night. While the program was in progress I walked out to the hallway of the school where it was being held. A well dressed middle aged man approached me and identified himself as the principal of the school. He asked me if I knew anything about this activity. I told him that I had helped with many of these events. Then he said, "They don't pray at these events, do they?"

Before I could answer him, they called me to come as it was time for me to speak. All of the teens were seated on the gym floor, and Jim was introducing me as I made my way to the microphone where he was. As I passed him, I said, "Check on that man in the door and see if you can occupy him while I speak. He could be a potential problem." That is all I had time to say.

I brought a gospel message and then prayed and led the young people in a step-by-step invitation to trust Christ. Just then the principal looked in the door. Over 100 had responded to the gospel invitation and come forward to be counseled by our trained counselors. The principal was not pleased; we received a letter the next week, saying we could never rent their school building again because of our praying and preaching. Praise the Lord for all of those who made decisions for Christ that night. This was the only time I ever knew of anything like that happening.

We held other events called 'Bowlathons', where young people bowl and skate all night. 'Operation Nightmare' was an event every night for two weeks, usually in the fall of the year, where we advertised with a hearse that had a sign on top that read, "Do not come if afraid of the dark, background of hysteria, heart condition, not a teenager." After a procession through town, led by a police car and a hearse, we ended up at destination unknown; then we went down a scary trail through the woods, and into a dark gym with a dimly lit casket down front. Then one of the leaders told some scary stories that ended with the corpse (one of our leaders) getting out of the casket in a jerky manner. The teens always thought we couldn't scare them, but we always did. Some of the biggest boys would often be so spooked they would try to climb the walls. Then, we would turn the lights on and hear testimonies and preach the gospel. This type of event would usually bring out some of the rougher type teens, and thousands of them made decisions for Christ over the years at 'Operation Nightmares.' One night near Cleveland, Ohio we had 2100 attend one of these events.

Our staff held evangelistic events with several thousand in attendance at Cedar Point, Kings Island, and even took over Bob-lo Island (an amusement park) near Detroit. There were boat rides on the Ohio River with Jack Wyrtzen and Harry Bollback preaching. Before one of these events my medical doctor wanted me to have a gallbladder operation, but I postponed it until the activity was over. The next day I became sick with much pain and Yellow Jaundice. I had surgery and ended up in the hospital for 21 days. It took a couple of months to regain my strength. That was not the best decision I ever made, but I was in charge and thought I had to be at this event.

For many years we were involved almost every weekend in one of these evangelistic events. We called them 'Roundups.' Some years I either organized or spoke at over 60 roundups. Some of these events we would need at least 50 people to help us. I pulled a small U-Haul with equipment and my family would go with me. On Sundays we would minister in churches. Some people have asked me, "Did you ever get tired?" If we did, I don't remember, because it was so much fun seeing people get saved.

"How then shall they call on Him in whom they have not believed? And how shall they believe in Him of whom they have not heard? And how shall they hear without a preacher? And how shall they preach unless they are sent? As it is written: How beautiful are the feet of those who preach the gospel of peace, Who bring glad tidings of good things!" Romans 10:14-15 NKJV

Short-term Missions

In 1972, Thelma and I were invited by Wayne Lewis, the North East Regional Director for Word of Life, to go with him and 62 young people on a short-term mission trip to St. John's, Newfoundland. We stayed in a Catholic school building and ate at a hospital cafeteria. The opportunities for ministry in churches, five day clubs, open-air evangelism, radio and TV appearances, and ministry to the young people who were with us, were fantastic. In fact, it was life-changing for us, as well as those who went with us.

Even though we were very active and satisfied in the Bible club ministry at the time, this trip left a desire in our heart to have more and more involvement in this type of activity. We not only continued to hear good results from people in churches in St. John's, but also we heard from the very people who were a part of the team that went with us. This is an excerpt from a letter I received on July 16, 1998.

Dear Brother Nicholes - "I would like to thank you personally for your involvement with Word of Life and for your faithful service to the Lord during these many years. I recall July 16, 1972 when your youth Reachout group ministered at First Baptist Church in St. John and, praise God, that morning I came to know Jesus as my personal Lord and Savior. This is my 26th spiritual birthday. I do thank the Lord for His faithfulness. I have never once doubted my salvation and have never looked back. My husband was saved the following Sunday, July 23, 1972. Together we have served the Lord at First Baptist Church since that time. God bless you and keep you in his service." - Love in Christ, F.S, Mount Pearl, Newfoundland

Seven years after our trip I met a young lady who had been one of the teens on the missions trip to St. Johns, Newfoundland. She was now the wife of a youth pastor in my area. She was still excited about all that happened in her life on that mission's trip. I made the statement that I wished there was a way I could find out what all the young people were doing who were on that trip. She said that she had stayed in contact with several of them, and she was sure many of them had stayed in contact with each other. She told me she would try to find out about what these young people were doing and report back to me. About six months later she got back to me and said, as nearly as she could find out, at least 50 of the 62, who went on that trip were either in full-time ministry or preparing for ministry. This only enhanced our desire to become more involved in short-term missions. We simply could not get it out of our mind.

Almost every year for 15 years, I would share my desire with Jack Wyrtzen my desire to do short-term missions again with Word of Life. Each time Jack would say that Word of Life already had too many irons in the fire to keep them all hot. Finally, one day I told my boss Paul Bubar that I still felt strongly that the Lord wanted Thelma and me to do this; and as much as I didn't want to leave Word of Life, we might have to in order to fulfill this desire. He told me to wait because he knew something I didn't know.

Soon I found out that he had been asked to become the

Overseas Director of Word of Life. He came to me and said, "Lou, do you still want to do that short-term missions thing?" Of course I said, "Yes." Then Paul told me Jack Wyrtzen had given his approval. He wanted me to turn the club ministry in the Midwest over to someone else and give my full time in starting and directing Reachout (short-term missions). I was thrilled, but surprised that I would be doing this full-time. I had envisioned doing this part-time and still doing Bible clubs.

Even though Jack was a long time in giving his permission, he was my strongest supporter once we started. Within a few hours after I would return from each trip, the phone would ring, and I would tell Thelma, "I bet that is Jack." Sure enough, it would be him wanting a report of what had happened.

Our first trip was to Kenya, East Africa, in 1998. It was amazing, but we had 62 young people, identical to the number we had on my first trip to Newfoundland. I always made a set up trip for arrangement of housing, transportation, food, ministry opportunities and so forth about six months before we would actually go. We would take 14-year-olds and up, which included the college-age for counselors. We also took adults as music directors, male and female counselors; and some of us would double as teachers in the classes we taught the teens along the way. Also, a couple of us would do the preaching.

We had meetings in public schools (sometimes two or three a day), churches, prisons, army bases, hospitals, youth rallies, and all types of open-air meetings. From the time the young people would sign up, we would coach and encourage them in their support raising. Our daughter Beth was my secretary and worked very hard at this. If we hadn't, I'm sure we would've had many get discouraged and drop out. We also helped them get their passports and visas and asked them to read a couple of books in preparation before coming to boot camp for a week of classes and training. We always practiced music, drama, soul winning, and counseling techniques. Derek DeCambra, a wonderful Christian from the

Metropolitan Opera in New York City, always came to help with the drama teams. Teachers at the Word of Life Bible Institute taught our counselors practical classes in preparation. We also had a couple of the fellows who carried and operated the sound system, as well as a video camera.

We always had a neat and different uniform we dressed in each year. Each trip consisted of one week of training and three weeks on the mission field. Some said the week of training was worth it even if they never went on the trip. The days on the trip were intense, and we often ministered long hours.

Many times we would split our time between two different countries. Most of the time was spent working with Word of Life missionaries already on the field. Sometimes we went to new fields exploring the possibilities of starting Word of Life in these countries. We tried to have one full day of sightseeing and shopping in each country and at least one fun time each week.

Of course, we often saw many sites as we traveled. We never had a day without having quiet time and family time where we shared from our quiet time and prayed for the activities of that day. We also had times of challenge from the Word and practical issues of the day. Every trip was different and provided different types of blessing.

The nearest I have ever been to true revival happened on one of our trips to Hungary. We had been in ministry all day and came back to the small village of Toalmas where we were staying at our beautiful Word of Life Castle. We had a meeting that night in a large building in the center of town and invited everyone in the town to come. The wife of the mayor came, and she made a decision for Christ along with several other prominent people in the community.

When we got back to the Castle, we had a praise and prayer meeting before going to bed as we often did. There was a lot of rejoicing, and then one of the young people got up and described what a phony he had been. He said he was over here on the other side of the world telling others about Christ and that he never witnessed to his unsaved family back home. He began to weep and ask God to forgive him. Then, one by one, others began to get up and asked God to forgive them for the way they treated their parents, for not witnessing to their friends, or for not being concerned about lost loved ones, and so forth. Every once in a while someone would start a hymn. Everything was spontaneous, and it was evident the Lord was in control of the meeting; it lasted for a couple of hours. It was getting late, and I knew we had to get up early the next morning for more meetings; so I stood up and told them I hated to stop the meeting but we also needed some sleep. I prayed and told them to go straight to their cabins and lights out. We, as leaders, stayed behind for a few minutes rejoicing and praising the Lord for the mini- revival we had just experienced with these young people. It was certainly nothing that we had planned and evident that the Lord had met with us. When we left the building, we found the young people still outside in prayer groups praying and singing. It took us a while, going to each prayer group and persuading them we had better get some sleep so we could give the Lord our best the next day. It was definitely an experience none of us will ever forget.

In 1989, we went to Australia and New Zealand. We had 100 sign up for that trip. We were thrilled to have so many, but we decided that 75 junior and senior high teens were our maximum to handle on one trip. The Lord gave us close to 75 several times after that. We didn't want to turn any away, so we took the last 25 to register on a trip to Carosou when we got back from Australia. It was a smaller team, but God blessed in a wonderful way as we lived in a rustic camp site and ministered with Calvin Varlock and our Word of Life missionaries in that country.

"But you shall receive power when the Holy Spirit has come upon you; and you shall be witnesses to Me in Jerusalem, and in all Judea and Samaria, and to the end of the earth." Acts 1:8 NKJV

Life Threatened

In 1995, my wife and I were on a ministry trip to South, Korea. During this time, we were heading up Word of Life's short term missions program called 'Youth Reachout.' We were in the planning stages of taking a group of 75 young people to Papua New Guinea the following summer of 1996. I decided to leave my wife in Korea and take a brief trip to Papua New Guinea to set up for this mission trip the next summer.

I had never been to Papua New Guinea before, and I didn't know anyone in that country. Before making plans for this mission trip I had heard there was a graduate of our one year Word of Life Bible Institute in Australia who was a native of Papua New Guinea. He was then doing evangelistic work in Papua New Guinea. He didn't have a car or a phone, so I contacted a Christian bookstore in Port Moresby, which is the capital of Papua New Guinea, and asked them if they happened to know John Airi. They said they did as he often came into the bookstore, and they would deliver a fax to him the next time he came. I immediately sent him a fax asking if he would be willing to help me set up a two-week mission trip in his country with 75 young people. He replied that he would be delighted to help me, and we corresponded back and forth by fax through the bookstore.

I decided to take this advance trip from Korea to Papua New Guinea to meet John and to set up for the mission trip. I took a night flight from Seoul, Korea to Port Moresby, Papua

New Guinea, and arrived there about 7 a.m. I proceeded through customs. When I went to the waiting room, I had no idea of what John looked like. However, since I was the only American on the plane John came right to me and introduced himself. He was excited about a place he had found for our group to stay when we came and wanted to show it to me right away. He said he had a friend waiting in his van outside to take us there. I had made arrangements to stay at the New Tribes guest house for the next couple of nights. I told him I would like to go first to New Tribes, wash up, and drop off my suitcase. He agreed, and we were on our way. That stop took about an hour, and then we drove across the city of Port Moresby, past the University, and out into the country. Before long we turned to the right. We traveled up a lonely dirt road for two or three miles, and wound our way up a steep hill to a beautiful lodge. It was owned by the Catholics, but they had told John we could rent it for our teen missions group the next summer. We looked around, and it seemed ideal, but when I asked how many it would hold they said about 40. We had 75 coming so I told John I was sorry, but we needed to do some more looking.

We left and were driving back down the narrow dirt road when suddenly a masked man with a gun jumped out in front of us and motioned for us to stop. He had the gun pointed at the driver's head, so we stopped immediately. He raised the gun over our heads and fired it three times, possibly to convince us that it was loaded. He then pointed it at us, and told us to get out of the vehicle and leave the motor running. I was in the front seat with the driver, and John was in the back seat. As we were getting out he yelled at us to go to the back of the vehicle. John opened his back door and started for the back. As I was getting out the man with the gun was on the driver's side. As I was following John to the back, he reached in his back pocket and flipped his billfold into the weeds and brush. I thought maybe I should do the same; but when I glanced at the gunman he was looking right at me, so I decided against it. I even had my passport sticking out of my shirt pocket.

About that time another masked man appeared with a bundle of rope. The man with the gun kept yelling at us to get to the back, as he pointed the gun at first one, and then another, with his hand on the trigger. He seemed very nervous; and then all at once he pointed down the road in the direction we'd been coming from and told us to run. We started running and glancing over our shoulders as we ran. I expected him to mow us down any minute.

(Some people have asked what I was thinking at that point.) I'm sure many things were running through my head, but the one thing I remember was wondering how my wife, Thelma, would ever find out what happened to me. When we had run about 300 feet we heard a scurry in the gravel. The two men had jumped into the vehicle, and were driving off, leaving us standing in the middle of the road.

The first thing we did was have a prayer meeting; we thanked the Lord we were still alive. We also concluded that the Lord must still have something for us to do. Then we started walking up the road, and John retrieved his billfold from the brush. We walked another mile or so, and there was a stone quarry back off the road where they were crushing rock for the road. We stopped to ask if they had a phone, and they asked us why we were walking. We told them we had just been held up and our van was taken from us.

They asked where it had happened. When we told them they said we were lucky, because just a week earlier two policemen had been killed at about the same spot. We called the police station, and in a few minutes two or three jeeps arrived with several police, each with high-powered rifles. They drove up and down the road and through the fields, but they found nothing. Then they loaded all of us into the jeeps and took us to the police station where the van driver filled out some papers about the stolen vehicle. The van driver then called his brother, who came and drove us back to Port Moresby.

The next day was Sunday, and I spoke at a church. When I began, I told the people I had just arrived in Papua New Guinea the day before and that I had received a "royal welcome". I told them how we had been held up and our vehicle taken from us. Then I preached a message and gave an invitation. As soon as the service was over, a young man came forward from the back of the church and asked me where this holdup took place. When I told him we went out past the University and up a dirt road, he said, "I know who did that." He said he had only been saved about a month, and that he had previously been a member of that group. They were called 'The Rascals.' I said, "They are rascals, all right." Then he told me he thought he could get the van back. I said, "That would be great!" He said he would go that afternoon and try to get it. When he came back later he reported that he found one of the Rascals and asked if he knew anything about the van. He said he did, but he couldn't tell him where it was, or he would be killed.

When I came back to the States, I kept asking John by fax if he had heard anything more about the van. John kept telling me "No", but finally one day he wrote and said the Rascals had sent him a note and told him where the van was and where he could find the keys. He picked up the van, and it didn't have a scratch on it. When we went back for the mission trip with the young people a few months later we used the same van again.

This experience convinced me that we needed to find a place to stay that had high security. God led us to a nice motel near the airport with a high barbed wire fence around it, guards at the gate, and guards at the entrance of the motel. Also the manager was a Christian, and gave us a terrific discount. Each morning for two weeks John and a pastor friend brought all 75 of us our breakfast to the motel.

We had a great ministry every day at the public schools, the University, street meetings, and churches. We would go to a park, and before we could get out of the bus and set up the equipment, two or three hundred people would be gathered to hear us. The young people would sing, present drama, give their testimonies, and one of us would bring a gospel message. Several hundred people came to know Christ while our group was there.

John Airi and I got to know each other well during these two weeks, and he began to ask me how he could become a part of Word of Life. I challenged him to come to our Bible Institute in New York and to study the Word of God for one year and learn more about ministry. That is what he did, and at the end of his training, he became a missionary on our staff. After raising his support here in the States, he returned to Papua New Guinea. He started developing a staff, and he has been our Word of Life director in that country.

> *"And the things that you have heard from me among many witnesses, commit these to faithful men who will be able to teach others also."* II Timothy 2::2NKJV

Farm Boy Goes to Russia

In the early days of black-and-white television, I remember watching the top leaders of the Kremlin stand on the reviewing stand (located on top of Lenin's tomb in Moscow) as the Soviet tanks and huge armor-bearing equipment rolled across Red Square in a show of force. Never in my wildest dreams did I ever think that one day I would stand in that very place and preach the gospel!

When we returned from our Youth Reachout trip to Australia in 1989, Jack Wyrtzen was telling people we would be going to Russia with Youth Reachout teams. I was thinking, "What in the world would we do in Russia where they put people in jail for preaching the gospel?" At that point the Cold War was on, and Bibles had been forbidden for 70 years.

Little did I realize that three years later the Iron Curtain would be down, and Youth Reachout would be heading out to Russia with over 70 teenagers. Yes, the Iron Curtain was down, and the doors of opportunity were wide open! Our missionaries in Germany helped us plan a missionary outreach that was unbelievable! The Lord made it possible for us to go places and do things I would have never imagined.

When communism fell the Communist Party didn't need their cultural halls, so we were able to rent these big halls that would hold 3000 people for $40 per night. These cultural halls were like huge theaters with a very large stage and an orchestra pit. We rented them night after night in different cities and packed them out. Most of the people didn't come to hear the gospel. They came to see these Americans that they had been told for many years were terrible. They had even been told that Christians in America offered up their children as a sacrifice.

The Christians who helped us plan this missions outreach said, "Don't bother to come unless you have a two-hour program." Our young people provided musical groups as well as instrumental numbers. We had several drama teams, and various young people gave their testimony each night, some telling how they trusted Christ at a very early age. Then we preached a simple salvation message with an invitation.

At the invitation we asked first for a show of hands of those who wanted to pray with us to be saved. Then if they prayed the prayer and meant it we asked them to stand to their feet; and then if they really meant their decision to come to the stage as a testimony before the whole crowd. So many stood to their feet the first night that I couldn't believe they understood, so I asked the interpreter to have them sit down.

As I went through the invitation again, the same amount stood once more. So we brought them forward, and they filled the stage. We didn't have nearly enough counselors or interpreters to help those making decisions. As a result we took them in groups and explained what Christ had done for them on the cross of Calvary; and now if they had sincerely asked Jesus to save them, He had heard them and given them what they asked for (I John 5:14-15).

Afterwards we gave each of them a copy of the Word of God. For most of them this was the first Bible they had ever held, and many of them hugged it and wept. We repeated this several nights in different cities, and there were between 250 and 500 that came forward each night. One night there were 750 that came forward. It was such a humbling and moving experience just to see the power of God at work in the lives

of these people who had been told for so many years that
there was no God and were even forbidden to have a Bible.

Other opportunities we had on that trip allowed us to
go right into the public schools, army bases, and prisons to
present programs and share the gospel. We spoke at an Army
base where the cosmonauts trained for their first flight to the
moon. They told us that we were the first Americans allowed
on their base after the fall of communism.

Our young people sang, testified, and presented drama
every place we went. Then we would preach a simple salvation message, give an invitation, and many would come
forward to accept Christ. I remember being in a meeting in
a large hospital one night, not far from where the Chernobyl
nuclear accident had happened. Death was written on the
faces of people of all ages, and we realized that for many
they probably would never have an opportunity to hear the
gospel again.

We were welcomed into the public schools to share the
Word of God freely with the students. It was so soon after the
fall of communism that I remember in one school seeing a
teacher going around ahead of us taking down the pictures of
Lenin that had been required to be posted in every classroom.
One day we drove our two buses into the heart of Moscow
where we put on a rally in Red Square. We brought our sound
system and set it up right in front of Lenin's tomb. Also, in
front of us was the guard who constantly marched back and
forth between the tomb and the Kremlin gate. There was a
long line waiting to get inside to view the body of Lenin,
preserved there under glass.

With this all going on we held a gospel rally. When we
gave the invitation many knelt on the pavement, weeping
and making a profession of faith in Christ. We gave them
all Bibles, and many of them hugged their new Bible and
thanked us for them. Sometimes we would stop our buses
when we saw a crowded train or subway station, and we

would pass out Bibles and gospel literature. Then we would explain the Roman's Road, or other verses on the plan of salvation, with the whole group and have them turn to the page in their Bible and go through the verses with us.

All of the Bibles we gave out had Russian on one side of the page and English on the other. Because of this, our young people could look at it in English and point across the page to Russian as they explained it through an interpreter. We had several thousands of these Bibles printed in Russian on a printing press that had been used by the Communist Party to print their propaganda. When the Iron Curtain fell, it was obtained by a Christian organization to print Bibles; and we were able to get them printed for $.78 per Bible.

With 75 English-speaking young people on our team we needed several interpreters. We could not find enough Russian interpreters who knew the Lord, so we hired some unsaved college students to travel with us. We always used the dedicated Christians to interpret the message in our meetings, but used the unsaved when our teams were witnessing one-on-one with people. After traveling with us for three weeks, several of these interpreters made a salvation decision just translating the message of salvation and reading Scripture over and over. However some translators didn't get saved. The amazing part was to see how many people became Christians through the interpretation of His Word through these unsaved translators. Some of our young people would say, "If God can use an unsaved translator to lead people to Christ, I know he can use me as a missionary."

Several people have asked me how we did follow up with all of those who made decisions for Christ. I wish I could say we were able to channel all of these into a good gospel preaching church that welcomed them in and fellowshipped with them. However the churches we were able to work with were few, and most of them were small.

Our team was invited to come and conduct a program

at some of these churches on Sundays. I remember a couple of occasions when there was no way we could get into the church with the church people inside. So we just moved outside. Someone blocked off the street, and we conducted our meeting in the street. The church people would sit on the sidewalk and the edge of the street. This meant that there was no room in the churches for all of the people who got saved in our meetings, and if there had been, it was filled with old people, and not too conducive for the younger people to come. We were thankful we could lead them to Christ; however, many times we had to turn the names over to the church leaders and hope they would follow up the best they could.

Between 1992 and 1996, we made three trips to Russia with Youth Reachout, and it became harder to do ministry each time we went. The last trip we made we went to a smaller city several hours south of Moscow, and the government put more and more limitations on what we could and could not do. There was only a narrow window of time when we had freedom to do just about anything we wanted to do, and people were wide open to the Gospel. However it was a very exciting time to serve the Lord!

> *"Let the word of Christ dwell in you richly in all wisdom, teaching, and admonishing one another in Psalms and hymns and spiritual songs, singing with grace in your hearts to the Lord. And what-ever you do in word or deed, do all in the name of the Lord Jesus, giving thanks to God the Father through Him."* Colossians 3:16-17 NKJV

Family Ministry

Without a doubt the greatest and most challenging part of my ministry in the past 50 years has been my own family. When Thelma and I first got married we really had no idea of how to raise godly children so we cried out to the Lord for help and He really did help us. We both held college degrees but had never attended classes on how to love my wife, how to respect my husband or how to raise our children to love God and serve Him. These very basic teachings of life are sadly missing in the society in which we live.

I have felt for many years that no matter what type of ministry you may be involved in, there is no ministry more important than the ministry to your own family. I remember hearing Billy Sunday's wife, "Ma Sunday," speak many years ago. She said, "We ministered to people all over the world and missed our own family."

The Lord has certainly blessed me with an exciting life and a fulfilling ministry that has spanned the globe. However, none of this compares with the joy of seeing our children walk with the Lord, and we are privileged parents because of the Lord's saving grace and special blessing.

We are often asked what we did as a family. When our children were growing up in our home, we were busy in a growing, fast-paced ministry that was very demanding and rewarding. We certainly can't claim any special talents or abilities as parents. Any success that we have had is not because of us, but because of Him and His working in us and through us. We did try to pattern our home life and ministry as much as possible according to our understanding of His Word.

I remember soon after we started in the Bible club ministry I received a phone call from Jack Wyrtzen, and he asked how the family was and how the ministry was going. Then he said, "Lou, what did you get out of your quiet time today?" There was a long pause on the phone because I had not had a quiet time (personal time in the Word). He didn't reprove me, but simply said, "Let me share with you something I got from the Word today." Here I was trying to start a new ministry with young people, helping them establish godly habits of Christian living, and I didn't even have a quiet time myself. God used this to help me see what a hypocrite I was. I coveted with the Lord that day that I wasn't going to let that happen again. I knew that if I didn't do it first thing each morning, I would get busy doing other things; and the day would pass, and there would be no quiet time.

So, for the past 50 years, I've been jumping out of bed every morning, splashing some water on my face, and then spending time in His Word. I decided that the breakfast table would be a good place to share with each other what we got out of our quiet time, and pray together. When our children were old enough to read and write, I gave them a Quiet Time Diary and asked them to read the Bible passage, write out in a couple of sentences what they understood the writer to be saying and a sentence or two on how they could make an application in their life. Then when they came to the table for breakfast they were to be prepared to share something using this method.

We called this our "Family Time" and we have been doing this at our house for over 45 years. It takes us through the Bible every six years and each person writes his own commentary on the whole Bible. As the dad I began to dig a little deeper each day and fill the page of a legal pad with my thoughts. It was such a blessing to our family that I decided to print it out, in a small booklet, each month and send it to all of my Club leaders, which I did for many years. Eventually, we asked a web designer to develop a web site and today you can go to www.Family-Times.Net and read it every day or sign up to have it come into your e-mail every morning.

I realized that we didn't know much about raising a family, so we started searching for Scripture verses that tell husbands, wives, and children their role in the home. When we found a verse, we put it on a card and memorized it. This way, we learned each other's role in the family. Finally, we printed these on cards, put them in a plastic jacket, and called them "Memory Verses for Happy Homes." Over the years we have not only worked on them ourselves, but given them to newly married couples. After that we did a "Christian Character" verse pack and eventually a "Soul Winners" verse pack that they used at the Word of Life Bible Institute, in their Evangelism class for many years.

Another thing that Thelma and I decided before we got married was that she would not work outside of the home for pay, unless I became physically disabled. This enabled her to take care of my needs and help me greatly in the ministry. Then when the children came along, she was always there when they needed her. She has always been my greatest helper and the greatest asset in the ministry the Lord has given to me.

I have always traveled a lot in the ministry and often had to be away from home. I determined early on that I would try to be at all of the activities I possibly could that my children were involved in to cheer them on. My boys loved to play basketball, and I don't think I missed many home games. I also arranged my schedule to take my children out to breakfast one-on-one, every couple of months as long as they were home. I still do, when I get a chance to do it. I would take them to whatever restaurant they wanted to go to, and then told them we would talk about whatever they wanted to talk about. Sometimes we would spend two or three hours of quality time together.

When our children became old enough to do things in the ministry, I tried to get them involved with me. I took them with me to the many evangelistic roundups we had scheduled throughout the year, and they were able to see the tremendous response to the preaching of the gospel. I often spoke in churches on the weekends, and I would always tell the pastor what we could do as a family, if he would like to use us. Thelma often spoke to a ladies' Sunday school class. In his latter teen years, Steve would speak to the teens. Mike was a ventriloquist, and he would be used in the children's classes, and Beth played the cow bells. Then I would preach, and we would all come home rejoicing in how the Lord had used us as a family.

It was not always easy to keep our priorities straight. My boys attended a Christian school, and they played on the basketball team. At the beginning of the season, we would give the coach our ministry schedule so he would be aware of times they would not be available for games. They were good players, so he always wanted them to play when they were available. However, when game time rolled around, and they were not able to be at a certain game because we had ministry scheduled, he would put pressure on by saying they would lose the game if our boys didn't play. Sometimes it wasn't easy to keep the coach happy and the ministry at the top of the priority list.

When our children were small, we tried to teach them the value of money. We did not think that giving our children an allowance was a good thing because it was teaching them to expect to get something for nothing. ("If a man doesn't work, he shouldn't eat.") Instead, we would pay them for certain jobs we had them do. When they were little, we had three jars for each of them to place their money. The first jar held the 10% that was for the Lord, the next held 10% for them to keep, and then 80% was to be kept for their college education. This was what we called the 10-10-80 plan. The only money they could spend was the 10% they could keep. We told them they could spend this on ice cream, candy, and so forth; but if they saved it, they could get a bicycle or something else they might like.

As they got older we helped them earn more money, but still using the 10-10-80 plan. As an example, when the boys were 13 or 14, I set them up in the firewood business. They cut up firewood, advertised it in the newspaper, and we had a trailer to deliver it. They did everything except drive the car to deliver it, and when they were 16 and had their driver's license, they did that.

They also worked in our print shop after school and on Saturdays punching and binding Quiet Time Diaries, which we paid them to do. For our daughter, Beth, we had her help us in the office. We raised a large garden, and she also sold produce. They were all able to save up enough so that combined with working while going to college, they were able to pay for their college education and graduate debt-free. We didn't pay for their college education, but we always paid for their transportation to come home at Christmas and vacation times.

Concerning our children's education, we decided not to send them to preschool or kindergarten because we wanted to spend that time with them, training them. We always told them that we expected them to go to elementary school, junior high, and senior high school, and the Word of life Bible Institute for one year. After that, they could choose whatever college they wanted to attend. Each of our children chose a different college, but we were very pleased with the choice each one made. Steve went to Liberty, Mike went to Tennessee Temple and Beth went to Baptist Bible College.

"Train up a child in the way he should go,
And when he is old he will not depart from
it." Proverbs 22:6 NKJV

83

Asked to be Asia Representative

Have you ever heard it said that life doesn't begin at 40 for those who run like 60 when they are 20? I don't know about that, but I do know that it makes me tired now just looking at the schedule I use to keep when I was in the prime of my ministry. However, if I had another life to live I probably wouldn't be able to get everything done that I wanted to do. At the same time I know that if I still had three lives to live it is only the things done for Christ that will last.

The first two areas of ministry (Bible club and Youth Reachout) that the Lord allowed us to be a part of in Word of Life, were something we sought. We definitely felt led of the Lord to these two areas of ministry. When our Executive Director, Joe Jordan, asked us to be the representatives for Word of Life Asia, we were surprised, but honored, as our three children and their families were involved in ministry with Word of Life in that part of the world.

Our oldest son, Steve, was the Northeast Asia Director; our second son, Mike, was the Director of Bible Clubs and Camps in South Korea; and our daughter Beth, and her husband, Chris, were soon to open up a new School of Youth Ministry in English in Taiwan. I had already been traveling to different Asian countries doing ministry, so had many acquaintances there. Realizing that over 60% of the world's population is located in Asia and less than 10% of all missionaries in the world are ministering there, I was challenged to the task.

We immediately started making trips to China, India, Taiwan, Myanmar, Thailand, Cambodia, Hong Kong, and etc. Because of their huge populations, we were especially challenged to China and India. I was invited by Dr. T.E Koshy, Chaplain at Syracuse University, to go with him to Hyderabad, India, to speak at a three-day youth conference consisting of 15,000 young people ages 15 to 25.

Dr. Koshy was from India and had great contacts there. This invitation to speak reminded me that I was the same high school student that skipped taking a class in public speaking because I was afraid to stand up in front of anyone and say anything. This was certainly a miracle of God!

To stand before such a large crowd of young people and preach several times was a unique opportunity. Many of these young people had traveled many hours on foot or public transportation to get there and arrived with just a paper sack of clothing and articles for this three day conference that was held in a very large tent. They always took off their shoes and sandals and threw them into a pile, outside the tent, before they came in. I never could figure how they found their own shoes when they left. I never obtained enough courage to put mine in the pile, but carried them with me.

The fellows sat on one side of the tent and the ladies on the other side with their heads covered. Everyone sat on the ground. The meetings consisted of one hour of singing, one hour praying, and one hour for the message. They started about nine o'clock in the morning and ended about nine o'clock at night.

At the meals, they all sat on the ground in lines facing each other, with about 5 feet between the rows. All their meals consisted of rice and curry which had been prepared on an open fire. It was served with precision. One person in each line laid a large leaf down in front of each person. Right behind this person, another one came with a basket of rice and put one large scoop on each leaf. Then a person came with a bucket of curry and put a dipper of curry on the rice. They all waited until everyone was served and someone thanked the Lord for the food before they ate with their hands. When finished, they threw the leaves in a barrel and washed their hands under a line of water spigots.

One hour of siesta was next, and then they came back for a duplicate of the schedule in the morning. The same process was repeated for the evening meal, and then they came back for three hours in the evening. You might think they would get very tired, but if they did, they didn't show it. They always looked very attentive and took notes as all the messages were translated by an interpreter. An invitation was given each day, and several accepted Christ as Savior; and hundreds made dedication decisions.

I made four trips to India, and it was something I will never forget. I made five trips to China and had different experiences each time. On my last trip, I was introduced to a pastor who has six kindergartens and six churches he started in Hong Kong. He reaches the parents for Christ through the kindergartens and then starts a church. He now has two kindergartens and two churches in mainland China. He has offered to build a building for us and will help us start a "Word of Life" School of Youth Ministries in English under his umbrella.

Almost everyone in China wants to learn English. We invited this pastor to come and visit our camps and Bible Institute in New York, and he came and met our leaders. We hope to have a team of missionaries going to *China* soon. Just think of the potential since China has the fastest growing church in the world!

We now have a Word of life Bible Institute on Jeju Island, South Korea, with students coming from all over the world. Since the Bible Institute is all in English and those who attend must be Christians, the best place to draw students from are the Schools of Youth Ministries in English in other Asian countries. Many college-age students are saved and discipled through the schools because of their great desire to learn English. I believe Word of Life could have many SYME's in China, India, Hong Kong, Taiwan, Myanmar, Cambodia, Thailand, Japan, Korea and other Asian countries. We just need more new missionaries to help establish the schools.

I have made trips to all of these countries over the past 10 years making contacts and planting seeds for this to happen. From these discipleship schools, I believe we can eventually establish camps and Bible clubs where we do not already have them. Since most of the teaching is in conversational English, and the teachers are recruited from the U.S. and Canada, Thelma and I have spent a lot of our time recruiting retirees and college grads that are looking for a short-term mission's experience. It presently takes between 50 and 60 teachers per year to fill these needs. When in these countries, we speak in churches, conduct special family conferences, teach classes at SYME, speak in Chapel, speak at staff conferences, and act as a consultant with various staff members. We have also enjoyed spending some time with all of our children and grandchildren who are missionaries with Word of Life in Korea, Jeju Island, and Taiwan. At the time of this writing, I am 79 and Thelma is 75 years of age. We are in the process of selling our home in New York and building a dorm at the new Bible Institute on Jeju Island, South Korea. We already have our missionary visa and plan to move to an apartment on one floor of the dorm and be there to help in any way we can. It is our desire to stay busy as long as we can and finish well.

> *"I have fought the good fight, I have finished the race, I have kept the faith. Finally, there is laid up for me the crown of righteousness, which the Lord, the righteous Judge, will give to me on that Day, and not to me only but also to all who have loved His appearing."* II Timothy 4:7-8 NKJV

Dear Dad and Mom

(Written by our oldest son Steve after
he graduated from College)

As Kris, Teresa and I were coming home from our summer camp ministry we were talking about some of the kids and STC'ers who were either the children of parents who are Christian leaders or kids who had been raised in a "good Christian home." Kris asked me "Why is it that so many kids with a good Christian heritage do not have a heart (or desire - "want to") to do what is right?" My mind went back to a set of parents who believed raising their children should be on their highest priority list of important "things to do" . . . who believed it was important that a family should be a family and not just a house where five people come and go, stopping only for eating and sleeping . . . who had moral and Biblical values . . . who passed them on to their kids . . . who believed the promise in Proverbs 22:6 that a child properly trained will not go wrong. I will ever be grateful to the time and effort this set of parents put into their children for I am their oldest of three. This "set of parents" is my parents.

So why is it? "Why do so many kids with a good Christian heritage not have a heart (or desire - a "want to") to please God, doing what is right?" I have been raised in your godly home where I, Mike and Beth all have a desire to please God, to do what is right. This is not an instilled command we have had to follow, but one each one of us has individually chosen to do. You have trained us in such a way that we did what was right.

In our home we did not tell you what to do. If we wanted something, we would ask. Mom did not tell dad what to do she would ask him. And dad didn't run around the house just telling everyone to do this or that. Often he asked us what we thought . . . about what style house our family built, the color of carpet and walls, we went over the blueprints together . . . about how we should plant our garden . . . he wanted our input . . . this was our family. But it was understood in our house that dad had the final say. We learned not to "backtalk," we learned to obey. Dad believed in what we came to know as a **chain of command.** This is where we as children in the home were to obey you, where mother was to submit to dad's leadership and where dad loved each one of us in such a way that we wanted to do what he asked. Often, even in the homes of Christian leaders (many which we have been in), moms tell dads what to do and kids tell mom and dad what to do.

I can remember times in our home when we as children were just in the beginning stages of learning the unnatural habits of being obedient, truthful, and kind. During this time it was your **effective discipline** that helped us develop good habit patterns in our lives. You would let us know what you expected from us. You showed us from the Bible what kind of behavior was pleasing to God. You then would **instruct** us to conform to that style of behavior. If we were not obedient, honest, or kind you would then **warn** us of the corrective measures that would be taken if we again did wrong so we would do what was right. If we again did what was wrong you kept your promise and **correction** took place.

I do not believe you were simply concerned that discipline took place. You were equally or more concerned **how** you did discipline. I believe it was effective because you tried your best to have **A balance of love and control.** A big reason we were never the "prodigal" kids was that you used the rod. When we had done wrong and needed correction I can still remember how it was carried out.

(I would be asked to go to your room where I would wait about five minutes. One of you would come into the room, sit down with me at the foot of the bed and ask me "What did you do that was wrong? Did you understand what the penalty would be before you did wrong? I was then told that because you loved me very much you did not want me to be a guy who had a habit of doing what was wrong. And God had said the use of the rod brings wisdom.)

(I would bend over one knee where a firm 18 inch ruler or your very flexible belt would firmly be applied to my "seat of understanding." Between the pain of my wrongdoing and the pain of the belt or paddle I would soon cry and it was understood that the strikes would continue to come until I quit crying. I would then bend over your other knee where I was again spanked until I quit my crying. Then we would sit on the edge of the bed and talk. I would ask for your forgiveness and ask God to forgive me. You then hugged me and told me how that you loved me and was glad I was a part of your family. With a "new start" I was ready to start again.)

You never slapped us with your hand or disciplined us in anger that I can remember. You restrained us by using the rod. I knew that this wasn't just your idea because several verses were put to memory. "Chasten thy son while there is hope, and let not thy soul spare for his crying" (Prov. 19:18). "He that spareth his rod hateth his son: but he that loveth him chasteneth him many times" (Prov. 13:24). "Withhold not correction from the child: for if thou beatest him with the rod, he will not die" (Prov. 23:13). "The rod and reproof give wisdom: but a child left to himself bringeth his mother to shame" (Prov. 29:15). Never once was I beaten in anger nor show any scars for any correction I received. I believe many Christian parents do not discipline their children.

Many of those, who do, swat them once or twice, provoking them to anger instead of instructing, warning, and then in love correcting. The household of Eli, the priest of Shiloh, was cursed "because his sons made themselves vile, and he restrained them not." (I Samuel 3:13).

You believed it was important that a family should be and do things together and not just a house where five people come and go, stopping only for eating and sleeping. We did everything together . . . from gardening . . . to traveling . . . to ministering in churches . . . to office work . . . to eating . . . sharing quiet time . . . evening devotions . . . picking out a house . . . the color of the carpet . . . paint color for the walls . . . mowing the lawns . . . eating out . . . we did a lot together. There were family nights making soap, cheese, ice cream. I thought of how you placed it high priority, to be there when we were . . . playing basketball . . . playing a piano recital . . . participating in Teens Involved . . . hearing us preach or teach . . . Many times you were the only or one of the few parents who came. We have been family that spends **time together.**

Some of the times I remember most are the talks we had. The mornings with dad at Elby's or Bob Evan's. Talking about future plans . . . priorities . . . relationships . . . unwise trends. I think of the discussions we had traveling in the car. I remember one on the way to Quality Farm and Fleet. Where you listened, honestly tried to understand, to help interpret (not interrupt) my thinking, to help me process what I was thinking. Most parents I am acquainted with do not take this kind of time nor do they communicate with their children.

In my counseling at camp, I shared about being a disciple, referring to Paul - Timothy - faithful men - others. As I look at our family, I would say that you are the Paul that has taught Timothy (us as your children) to teach faithful men (our children and many others we come in contact with) to teach others (and the process never ends). As you shared what you heard this past week at the Moody Conference I know you have been a good example of parents who **pass your values on**, to us. You passed on Biblical values such as knowing, loving and glorifying God . . . being honest, being faithful . . . being successful as God measures it . . . being obedient . . . working hard. You also passed on personal values that our family followed such as how we dressed . . . how we handled our money . . . TV . . . movies . . . dating . . . You have done your best to be consistent in living by the values you believed in. Because of this most everything that is important to you has become important to me. And now I believe it is important to have Biblical and personal values and to pass them on in my generation.

I still remember you telling me "Steve, you are far ahead of where I was at your age. I'm not going to be surprised if your range of influence one day will be greater than mine but that is a primary goal in raising you. I don't mean to put pressure on you but I want you to be the best you can be . . . to reach your potential . . . to whom much is given much will be required." If I thought of it once I have thought a thousand times dreaming of what my future might hold. **You believed in me**. I believed I could do it and a big reason was that you told me so.

Please don't get me wrong and begin to think that I think you are perfect parents or that I have to agree with everything you have done. For between the lines I have written there have been hard times . . . times of hurting . . . times of discouragements . . . times of disappointments. But more than all the times you have made it hard on me I know growing up I have done more than my share of failing and making it very hard on you. As I reflect back, I really have a lot to be thankful for and if I had it to do all over again, if I could pick and choose - you would still be the mom and dad I would desire. We've been good for each other. Definitely you for me and possibly you will admit - me for you. There are not many things I value in this world but the inspiring influence you have had on me would not hold a price tag. Even though it has not been easy - thank you for letting me go from total dependence on you as a child as I am becoming more independent. I know you know this was your primary goal in raising me, but letting go has never been easy. Thank you for the times you have allowed me to struggle when you could have done it for me but I needed to learn and for the times giving me the freedom to fail. And thank you for the times when I was struggling and needed you that you were there. And thank you for struggling to discern when to let me do it alone or when to get involved.

So what have I said? I believe, (for whatever my opinion is worth) you were successful parents because in our house we knew who was in charge, because you sought and took specific steps to discipline us in love, because we spent time to talk and be together, because you had good Biblical values to pass on to us, and because you believed in us. If and when I become a parent I trust that I can be as good a parent to my kids as you have been to me.

As I returned from a good summer at camp . . . as I was asked why so many kids from "good" parents go wrong . . . as I did a lot of reflecting . . . tears came to my eyes. It reminded me of "He'll be Gone Tomorrow (An illustration you used many times in preaching)." Words fall short of expressing my thanks to you for being an excellent mom and dad. Thank you very much!

Comment

It is difficult to write an autobiography and tell many stories from a lifetime of experiences without using personal pronouns. However, it is only the Lord who could take a simple farm boy who had seldom traveled more than 20 miles from home until he was 20 years of age and have him end up ministering in 52 countries around the world. What an awesome privilege it has been for me to be included as one of His children, and travel through the life of experiences I have been able to share in this book. I guess the great apostle Paul sums it up best when he says, "For by the grace of God I am what I am".

My purpose for writing this book is to share how great, how powerful and how loving God really is, and not who I am, and what accomplishments I have been able to achieve in this life. It is my sincere desire that those who read this book will be asking God what He wants you to do in and through your life, and seeing that only the things done for Him will last.

If you read this book while I am still living would you pray that I will finish well in serving my wonderful Lord and Savior Jesus Christ. If I have already graduated to my heavenly assignment would you especially pray that my children, grandchildren and wonderful Christian friends in this life will give their all to knowing and serving the one who has given His all for us.

For More Information

If you would like to receive more information about other books and ministry resources produced by Lou Nicholes go to www.Family-Times.Net or order books at"

www.XulonPress.com
www.Amazon.com
www.ChristianBook.com
www.bn.com (Barnes & Noble)

Other Books by the Author

The Bible in a Nutshell - 2003
Mark - *The Master Servant* - 2003
Numbers - *Wilderness Wanderings* - 2004
Acts - *The History of Missions* - 2004
I & II Corinthians - *Letters of Correction* - 2004
Romans - *A Roadmap for the Christian Life* - 2004
Joshua - *Conquest of the Promised Land* - 2004
Hebrews - *Patterns for Living* – 2004
Job – *From Riches to Rags and Rags to Riches* - 2007
Luke - *The Perfect Man* – 2007
John – *Master Teacher* – 2010

Photos

Lou as a Baby

Lou Held by his Brother Wayne

Lou with his Dog, Spot

First Day of School

Lou with his Dad and Mother

Jr. High

High School Basketball

High School Graduation

Lou's Model A Ford at Age 16

The Family Farm

Army Days, 1954 - 1956

Chapel in Germany
We had great Bible studies every Sunday night.

Studying at Philadelphia College of
the Bible, 1958—1962

Thelma Duckels
We met at a prayer meeting
at Philadelphia College of the Bible.

Our Wedding - June 12, 1960
It was performed at
Duckels Bible Camp.

Honeymoon Cottage in Mexico - 2 Months

Jack Wyrtzen
Founding Director of
Word of Life Fellowship

Rent-Free Home
on a Farm in
Southern Ohio

Car Purchased with *S&H* and *Top Value* Stamps

Paul Bubar
Bible Club Director

Bible Club Staff
Midwest States

Speakers at Mid-West Leaders Conference

Message Time - Basketball Marathon

Evangelistic Events

Speaking at a Leadership Conference

Missions Trips
- 1 Week Training
- 3 Weeks Trip

Youth Reachout
First Trip

One of the first US groups allowed on a Soviet military base after the Iron Curtain fell.

Ministering in
Red Square
Moscow

Lou almost lost his
life on his first
survey trip to
Papua New Guinea.

John Airi became the
Country Director of
Word of Life PNG.

Weekend Family Ministry

Missions Display at Mission Conference

Don Lough, Executive Director of Word of Life with Lou

Banquet with Communist Party Leader in China

The Bollbacks, Theis & Nicholes celebrate their shared anniversaries.

Our Entire Family - All of them are serving the Lord in Asia.

CPSIA information can be obtained at www.ICGtesting.com
Printed in the USA
LVOW010434130213

319809LV00010B/105/P

9 781625 093486